GREATER THINGS:
UNVEILING 52 EPIC SECRETS OF LEADERSHIP FROM SCIENCE AND SCRIPTURE!

Dr. Heather Lyall

ISBN: 979-8-218-40091-0

Dedication

Fred Rogers taught a generation to "look for the helpers" during tragedies. As a Christian adult, I tend to "look for the Christian leaders." I prayed on it as I watched the news. I repeatedly asked God, "Where is our Martin Luther King, JR? Where is our Billy Graham? Where is our generation's Ronald Reagan, Abraham Lincoln, or Barry Goldwater?" His reply was simple: "I gave you a strong mind and heart. I blessed you with a good family and an education. You ask where the leaders are. I say, develop them."

This book is dedicated to the Christian Leaders of the next generation. I expect to see even greater things from you.

CONTENTS

FORWARD
(FOR CHURCH LEADERSHIP AND PASTORS)

GREATER THINGS IS tailor-made for youth groups, homeschoolers, or teens eager to hone their leadership skills. This book can be completed within a year by delving into one chapter per week. Throughout this journey, diligent teenagers will undoubtedly witness a notable enhancement in their leadership abilities. As their mentor, parent, or group leader, your role is pivotal in fostering and nurturing their burgeoning leadership skills.

Greater Things is designed to guide Christian youth to become tomorrow's leaders. The leadership skills within each chapter are grounded in scientific principles and Biblical teachings, rendering it a valuable asset for up to a decade. As your youth mature, discussions will evolve to reflect their growing awareness of their surroundings, community, and the life-altering decisions they'll face.

CHOOSING YOUR YOUTH GROUP LEADER:

Youth today require <u>nonjudgmental</u> leaders. These individuals have weathered life's storms and are unafraid to share their struggles and triumphs. Imperfection is not a hindrance but a testament to God's grace. Leaders should be open about their mistakes, drawing inspiration from biblical figures like Moses, King David, and Abraham, who made mistakes but had God's mercy.

Youth group leaders should have compassion, a positive attitude, and unwavering love. As a youth group leader, their primary objective should be to instill the knowledge of each member's significance in God's plan, irrespective of their flaws, choices, or past decisions.

Listening is paramount; so youth group leaders should be able to refrain from offering unsolicited advice unless requested. Instead, pose thought-provoking questions to encourage critical thinking and demonstrate your genuine interest in their experiences.

Finally, youth group leaders should be responsible for delegating authority and empowering youth group members to take the reins whenever possible. Encouraging their involvement in decision-making processes, whether organizing fundraisers, participating in community events, or any other initiative. Let them embrace leadership roles early, knowing your guidance and support are ever-present.

INSTRUCTIONS FOR HOMESCHOOLERS

THIS BOOK IS designed for homeschoolers to use each week. After finishing a chapter, take a break for a week to reflect on what you've learned about leadership. Because homeschoolers might not always have instructors, it's suggested that you read the entire chapter, even sections meant for instructors.

There are many discussion questions provided, but if you're not in a group, it's okay to only answer a few in your notes. Remember, the most important part of learning leadership is practicing the skills you've learned during the week.

Try to incorporate the skill into your daily life whenever possible. For example, if you learn about courage, challenge yourself to step out of your comfort zone a couple of times. Write about your experiences in the notes section.

INSTRUCTIONS FOR GROUP
LEADERS/INSTRUCTORS

THIS BOOK IS crafted to assist youth group leaders in nurturing leadership skills among today's Christian youth. Many of the youngsters in my youth group have grown up in the church, familiar with the timeless tales of our faith. As they transition into young adulthood, they must elevate these narratives and aspire to become impactful leaders driven by their Christian convictions. This book is tailored to facilitate that journey.

Comprising 52 chapters, each meant to be explored weekly, this book is exclusively available in hardbound format, designed to withstand years of use. The layout includes ample space for notes, encouraging personal reflections, and documentation of memorable activities. However, to preserve confidentiality and respect members' privacy, refrain from recording specific names or meeting details.

Each chapter follows a structured format, which includes a definition, relevant Biblical references, tips for developing the skill being studied, discussion prompts, and engaging activities to reinforce the lesson. The section labeled "Information for Instructors" includes barriers to mastering each leadership skill if they are not mentioned during the group discussion. These barriers are provided for reference during group discussions.

The teens in my own youth group assisted in the creation of this book. They are between the ages of twelve and nineteen. My group members stated that after a long day at school, they could not focus on listening to a passage for more than about ten minutes. If youth group members feel overwhelmed or overloaded, engagement levels with the group will decrease. The goal is to introduce the group to aspects of leadership and focus their young minds on one topic per week. Therefore, the instructor only reads the definition, Biblical references, and tips (if applicable) in the section and then will choose 4-5 questions based on the ages and maturity levels of the group members to start a group discussion. Answering general questions and discussing their experiences, thoughts, and feelings provides a great opportunity for learning and engagement. As a rule, keep the teaching part of the meeting as short as possible, and the discussion part as long as possible, and encourage everyone to participate. During times when individual focus is lacking, I encourage leaders to allow the group members to read the sections aloud.

Your youth group comprises the future Christian leaders and should be treated as such. Effective communication with younger individuals hinges on a foundation of trust. In our youth group, we uphold a single rule: confidentiality. What is shared within the group remains within the group, fostering an environment of trust between leaders and members. However, it's crucial to remember that in many states, youth workers are mandated reporters in cases involving physical, sexual, or emotional abuse, as well as threats of self-harm or harm to others.

Given the importance of fostering a relaxed atmosphere conducive to fruitful discussions, chapters are intentionally brief. Moving through the chapter quickly allows ample time for snacks, brainstorming fundraising ideas, planning outings, and indulging in group activities. After a long day at school, it's essential to encourage active participation and limit distractions like excessive phone usage. Lessons are supposed to be short but have a long-lasting impact.

Discussion questions and activities are provided as suggestions, aiming for quality over quantity to prevent sessions from feeling overly academic. Ensuring every member has a chance to contribute fosters inclusivity and enriches the group dynamic.

Active listening by the group leader is paramount, both within and outside group sessions. Being available to lend an ear when members seek guidance or simply need someone to confide in builds trust and strengthens bonds.

Treating youth with respect and dignity is imperative, and avoiding condescending language that undermines their maturity. Exercise discretion when offering advice, recognizing it as a testament to their trust in your guidance. Confidentiality should be upheld unless mandated reporting obligations come into play.

Collaborating harmoniously with fellow leaders is essential, fostering an environment of mutual support and shared responsibility. Embracing vulnerability and sharing personal experiences of growth and resilience underscores the human aspect of leadership, illustrating God's unwavering grace amidst our imperfections.

Leadership
Chapter 1

Definition

Leadership is when someone shows others how to do things positively. A leader listens to people, helps them, and makes decisions to achieve goals. They inspire others to work together and make things better. Leaders guide a team toward success, using their skills to make everyone better and stronger.

Leadership has between 200 and 850 definitions in the Scientific community and can not be measured. Yet, we all know when leadership happens because we recognize it. The scientific community may not be able to replicate leadership, but it is possible to define leadership characteristics and develop those skills in others.

Biblical References

In the Bible, there are numerous references to leadership, both in terms of exemplary leaders and the qualities expected of them. Here are a few key references:

Moses - Moses is one of the most prominent leaders in the Bible. He led the Israelites out of Egypt, received the Ten Commandments from God, and guided the people through their journey in the wilderness. His leadership qualities include humility, obedience to God, and a willingness to serve his people selflessly.

Joshua - After Moses, Joshua became the leader of the Israelites. He led them into the Promised Land, conquering various territories. Joshua demonstrated strong faith in God, courage, and determination in leading his people.

David - King David is often regarded as one of Israel's most significant leaders. He was chosen by God and anointed by the prophet Samuel. David exhibited bravery, righteousness, and a heart devoted to God. Despite his flaws, he was known for his repentance and reliance on God's guidance.

Nehemiah - Nehemiah served as a leader during the post-exilic period, overseeing the rebuilding of Jerusalem's walls. He exemplified prayerfulness, vision, determination, and organizational skills in rallying the people to work together towards a common goal.

Jesus - Jesus is the ultimate example of servant leadership in the Bible. He taught his disciples to serve others selflessly, lead humbly, and prioritize love and compassion. Jesus washed His disciples' feet to symbolize humble service and sacrifice, setting a profound example for all leaders.

These biblical figures and their stories provide valuable lessons and principles for leadership, emphasizing qualities such as faith, integrity, courage, humility, compassion, and servant-heartedness.

Suggested Questions: (Please limit to 4-5 questions pertaining to your group)

- What makes someone a good leader? What qualities should leaders have?
- Can you think of someone from history or in your life who shows or showed leadership qualities?
- Why is it hard to describe leadership using science? Even though it's hard to measure, we can still see when someone is a leader.
- Can you think of someone who might not be called a leader but still helps and inspires others?
- Talk about leaders from the Bible like Moses, Joshua, David, Nehemiah, and Jesus. What qualities did they have that made them good leaders?
- Can you think of other leaders from stories or real life who have similar qualities to the Biblical Leaders?
- What does it mean to be a servant leader, like Jesus washing His disciples' feet?
- How can leaders today show they care about others and serve them, just like Jesus did?
- What lessons can we learn about leadership from the stories of these people in the Bible? How can we use these lessons to be better leaders in our own lives, like at school or with friends?
- Why is being humble important for leaders? How does being humble help leaders work better with others and make good decisions?

INFORMATION FOR INSTRUCTORS

Barriers to developing leadership skills can vary depending on individual circumstances, but some common barriers include:

- Lack of Self-Confidence: Many individuals may need to be more confident about taking on leadership roles, which can hinder their willingness to step up and lead effectively.
- Fear of Failure: The fear of making mistakes or not meeting expectations can hinder individuals from taking risks and seizing leadership opportunities.
- Limited Experience: Inexperience in leadership roles or lack of exposure to leadership situations can make it difficult for individuals to develop and demonstrate their leadership skills.
- Poor Communication Skills: Effective communication is essential for leadership, and individuals who need help to express themselves clearly or assertively may find it challenging to lead effectively.
- Resistance to Change: Some people may resist stepping into leadership roles due to a fear of change or a reluctance to challenge the status quo.
- Perceived Lack of Support: A lack of support from peers, supervisors, or organizational

structures can ensure individuals' confidence in their leadership abilities and encourage them to pursue leadership opportunities.

- Unwillingness to Delegate: Leaders who need help to delegate tasks and responsibilities may become overwhelmed and unable to focus on strategic leadership functions.
- Limited Emotional Intelligence: Leaders need a high level of emotional intelligence to understand and manage their own emotions and those of others. Individuals with limited emotional intelligence may need help to connect with and inspire their teams effectively.
- Difficulty Building Relationships: Building strong relationships and fostering trust is crucial for effective leadership. Individuals who struggle to connect with others or build rapport may face barriers to leadership success.
- Unwillingness to Seek Feedback: Leadership development requires seeking feedback, reflecting on strengths and weaknesses, and continuously improving. Individuals resistant to feedback may need help to grow and develop as leaders.

Overcoming these barriers requires self-awareness, perseverance, a willingness to learn and grow, and support from mentors, coaches, or organizational leaders. This book is written so that individuals twelve and older can gain knowledge and experience in leadership skills. Enjoy learning!

SUGGESTED GAME: FOLLOW THE LEADER

1. Choose a Leader: Select one person to be the leader. This person will start by performing actions that the other players must imitate.
2. Start the Game: The leader begins by performing a simple action, such as hopping on one foot, clapping their hands, or waving their arms. Everyone else must follow and mimic the leader's actions as closely as possible.
3. Keep Following: The leader continues to perform actions, and the other players must imitate them. The actions can be as simple or as complex as you like, depending on the age and abilities of the players.
4. Rotate Leaders: After a set amount of time or when the leader decides, another player takes a turn being the leader. The new leader then starts performing actions for the other players to follow.
5. Add Challenges: To make the game more exciting, you can add challenges or variations. For example, you could have the leader perform actions while moving around the room, or you could introduce new actions that require balance, coordination, or creativity.
6. Have Fun: The most important thing is to have fun and enjoy the game together! Encourage laughter and silliness as players try to keep up with the leader's actions.

"Follow the Leader" is a great game for promoting teamwork, coordination, and creativity while also providing plenty of opportunities for physical activity and laughter.

Notes:

Courage
Chapter 2

Definition

COURAGE MEANS BEING mentally or morally strong when dealing with danger, fear, or challenging situations. It's about facing problems, uncertainty, or things that scare you.

Biblical References

Consider David, a young shepherd who faced the giant Goliath with just a sling and stones. His courage and faith helped him beat Goliath and become a hero (1 Samuel 17).

Shadrach, Meshach, and Abednego refused to bow to King Nebuchadnezzar's golden image. They were thrown into a fiery furnace but stayed faithful to God, coming out unharmed. Their courage during challenging times showed their trust in God (Daniel 3).

Queen Esther bravely spoke to King Xerxes to save her people, the Jews, risking her life. She used her position to stop a plan to harm them (Book of Esther).

Joshua led the Israelites into the Promised Land even though he faced other strong nations. His courage and obedience to God led to victory (Book of Joshua).

The Apostle Paul, despite hardships such as imprisonment, still spread the Christian message with unwavering courage (New Testament).

These Biblical stories show courage in different forms, like facing danger, standing up for beliefs, and trusting God.

Tips for developing courage:
- Face Your Fears: Identify and slowly deal with your fears.
- Set Small Goals: Break big challenges into smaller, easier goals.
- Practice Mindfulness: Pay attention to your thoughts and feelings.

- Challenge Negative Thoughts: Ask yourself if those bad thoughts are true, and think positive instead.
- Learn from Failures: Look at mistakes as chances to learn and do better.
- Surround Yourself with Support: Have people around who cheer you on.
- Educate Yourself: Knowing what you're up against helps you deal with challenging situations.
- Take the initiative: Go after opportunities that are outside your comfort zone.
- Celebrate Successes: Be happy about what you've achieved.
- Visualize Success: Imagine yourself getting through tough times.
- Practice Empathy: Try to understand what others are going through.
- Take Care of Yourself: Make sure you're okay, both physically and mentally.

Discussion Questions: (Please limit to 4-5 questions that pertain to your group)

- Can you think of a time when facing something scary helped you grow as a person?
- Why do you think it's vital to challenge bad thoughts when trying to be brave?
- How can learning from mistakes help you be more courageous?
- How does knowledge help you be brave?
- What stops you from being brave?
- Can you think of a time when you or someone you know had to be brave?
- Can you tell me how one of the Bible stories listed, or another Bible story, demonstrates bravery?
- Which tip for developing courage do you think you could try out?
- Can you think of something you're scared of and how you might start facing it?
- Why is it valuable to learn from mistakes or failures when trying to be courageous?
- Can you tell me about a time when you learned something important from a mistake?

INFORMATION FOR INSTRUCTORS

Barriers to having courage:
- Fear of Failing: Some avoid new things because they fear failing.
- Worrying About Others' Opinions: Fear of people judging them stops some from doing something different.
- Low Self-Esteem: Believing in yourself is essential for being brave.
- Staying in Comfort Zones: Some are afraid to leave their safe spaces.
- Lack of Support: Being brave with people encouraging you is easier.
- Past Bad Experiences: Bad stuff that happened before can make people scared to take risks.
- Fear of the Unknown: Some are scared of things they don't understand.
- Desire to Be Perfect: Fear of making mistakes can stop people from being brave.
- Following Society's Rules: Doing things differently from what others expect can be scary.
- Lack of Resources: Not having enough stuff can stop people from being brave.

Suggested Game: Sound Ball

Have the group stand in a circle. One person makes a sound—any sound—while also making a throwing gesture towards another person in the group. That second person then 'receives' the sound by catching the ball and then repeats the sound sent to them. Then, without hesitation, the first receiver sends a new sound to another person in the circle. Keep the sound moving quickly and boldly to get everyone involved.

Insider Tips:

- Encourage your group not to predict or plan what sound they'll make if the ball comes their way. It is better to receive the one sent and then send a new one that emerges of its own accord.
- Ensure that folks actively receive the sound sent to them before sending one out. It's a great affirmation to the sender and helps build a spirit of generosity.
- Add in variations as your group gets better with Sound Ball. Ideas are to play Name a City ball, name a Vegetable ball, names that start with m ball, and so on.

NOTES:

COMMUNICATION
CHAPTER 3

DEFINITION

COMMUNICATION IS THE way we share, get, and give information. It can be verbal, nonverbal, written, or visual. Please read the tips for active listening located at the end of this chapter. Your instructor may provide you with a copy.

BIBLICAL REFERENCES

In the past, prophets in the Old Testament, like Isaiah, Jeremiah, and Ezekiel, used verbal communication to speak for God. They told the people what God wanted them to know. Jesus also talked to people, like in the Sermon on the Mount. He taught about how to be good and live the right way (Matthew 5-7).

Sometimes, we can communicate without talking. In a story from the Bible, Jesus tells about the Good Samaritan who helped someone without using words. He showed love and care by helping a stranger (Luke 10:25-37).

Written communication is when we use words on paper. In the Bible, God gave Moses the Ten Commandments on a mountain (Exodus 20:1-17). These commandments tell us how to live a good and fair life.

Visual communication is when we show things. For example, in the Bible, there's a story about a bronze serpent (Numbers 21:4-9). People who looked at it were healed.

The book of Ezekiel contains vivid and symbolic visions described by the prophet. These visions, such as the vision of the heavenly chariot, use rich visual imagery to convey spiritual truths and God's glory (Ezekiel 1).

Not all communication is good. In the story of the Tower of Babel, people wanted to build a tower to reach the heavens, but it went against God's plan. God made them speak different languages, which caused confusion. This story teaches us about the power and consequences of communication (Genesis 11:1-9).

There's also a story about Joseph and his brothers. They didn't communicate well, and it led to problems. They sold Joseph into slavery because of jealousy. But later, they learned to communicate better, and Joseph forgave them. This story shows the importance of good communication and forgiveness (Genesis 37-50).

Here are some tips to communicate better:

- Listen Carefully: Pay attention when others are speaking. Look at them and nod to show you understand.
- Use Clear Words: Speak clearly and use simple words so everyone can understand you.
- Be Respectful: Treat others with kindness and respect, even if you disagree with them
- Ask Questions: If you don't understand something, ask questions to get more information.
- Share Your Thoughts: Don't be afraid to share your ideas and opinions. Your thoughts are important too!
- Be Patient: Wait for your turn to speak and give others a chance to talk.
- Use Eye Contact: Look at the person you're talking to. It shows you're interested in what they have to say.
- Use Body Language: Use your body to show how you feel. Smile when you're happy and use gestures to express yourself.
- Stay Calm: If you feel upset or angry, take a deep breath and stay calm. It's easier to communicate when you're relaxed.
- Practice: The more you communicate with others, the better you'll become. Don't be afraid to practice talking to different people!

Remember, communication is about understanding and being understood. These tips can help you communicate better with friends, family, and classmates.

The key to communication is to make sure we use clear and simple language, be aware of different cultures, and pay attention to how we are feeling and how others might be feeling when we talk to them. It's important to make sure everyone is on the same page so we can understand each other better.

Discussion Questions: (Please limit to 4-5 questions that pertain to your group)

- What is the best way you have found to communicate thoughts and ideas?
- How do verbal, nonverbal, and written communication play a role in our daily lives?
- How does technology impact the way we communicate today?
- How can empathy improve communication?
- Can you think of a situation where understanding someone else's perspective would have helped in resolving a problem?
- Can you think of a time when someone used words to tell an important message like the prophets did in the Bible?
- How did Jesus show love and care without using words in the story of the Good Samaritan?
- Why was it important for Moses to receive the Ten Commandments in writing? How did it help people understand what God wanted them to do?
- How did the Tower of Babel story teach us about the problems that can happen when people don't communicate well?
- Which tip for better communication do you think is the most helpful, and why?
- Why is it important to be respectful and patient when we talk to others, even if we don't agree with them?
- How does asking questions help us understand each other better when we communicate?
- Can you think of a time when you used body language, like smiling or nodding, to show how you were feeling when talking to someone?

Information for Instructors:

Challenges:

- Physical Challenges: Sometimes, being far away from someone or dealing with a lot of noise can make it hard to talk and understand each other.
- Words and Meanings: Using difficult words or phrases that people don't understand or speaking in a way that's different from what someone is used to can create confusion.
- Feelings and Thoughts: Sometimes, our emotions or what we think about a person can get in the way of understanding what they are saying.
- Cultural Differences: People from different places might have different ways of talking or understanding things, and this can create barriers.
- Organizational Issues: When there are too many rules or levels of authority at work, it might be hard for people to talk openly. Also, getting too much information at once can be overwhelming.
- Technology Problems: If the tools we use to communicate aren't working well, or if we rely too much on technology, it can be tough to get our messages across.
- Personal Challenges: Not paying attention or feeling defensive can make it hard to have good communication.

Suggested game: Charades

Begin with a bowl of phrases and/or titles. In turn, each player draws a slip from the bowl and acts out the phrase shown using hand signals and body motions but no spoken words. Players then try to guess the title/phrase.

Insider tip:

- There are many online tools for choosing charade words, phrases, or titles.
- Do not allow teens to choose their own words and phrases to act out; even church youth groups can sometimes behave inappropriately.

Here are some suggestions for communicating: *Please make copies of this page for your group.

Listen Actively:

- When someone talks, pay attention.
- Let them finish before you speak.
- Show you're listening with your body and words.

Speak Clearly:

- Use simple and clear words.
- Check if the other person understands.
- Ask questions if needed.

Watch Your Body Language:
- Be aware of how you use your body.
- Look interested; use friendly gestures.
- Keep eye contact, but not too much.

Understand Others:
- Try to feel what others feel.
- Say you understand their feelings.
- Be supportive and caring.

Stay Calm:
- Keep control of your feelings.
- Take a break if you're upset.
- Don't yell or act aggressively.

Pick the Right Time and Place:
- Find a quiet place to talk.
- Choose a good time when you can focus.
- Make sure it's private for personal talks.

Use "I" Statements:
- Talk about your feelings using "I."
- Say "I feel" instead of blaming others.
- It helps avoid arguments.

Ask Questions:
- Ask questions to understand better.
- Use open-ended questions for longer answers.
- It keeps the conversation going.

Give Feedback:
- Say how someone can improve, not just what's wrong.
- Be specific and helpful.
- Be open to feedback from others.

Be Open to Feedback:
- Welcome advice from others.
- Learn from feedback to get better.
- Don't get upset; see it as a chance to grow.

Say Positive Things:

- Notice and praise good communication.
- Encourage others to communicate well.
- It makes talking easier.

Respect Other Cultures:

- Understand that people from different cultures may communicate in various ways.
- Respect those differences.
- Learn from each other

NOTES:

INTEGRITY
CHAPTER 4

DEFINITION

INTEGRITY MEANS BEING honest and sticking to strong morals and values. It's about consistently doing the right thing. Having integrity builds trust and creates positive environments at work, home, and school.

BIBLICAL REFERENCES

Ananias and Sapphira sold a piece of land and pretended to give all the money to their church, but they kept some for themselves. When caught, they faced serious consequences (Acts 5:1-11).

Judas Iscariot betrayed Jesus for money, leading to Jesus' arrest and crucifixion. Later, feeling guilty, Judas tried to return the money but ended up taking his own life (Matthew 26:14-16, 27:3-10).

Gehazi worked for Elisha, the prophet, but dishonestly took gifts from Naaman, a Syrian commander, for personal gain. As a result, he contracted leprosy from Naaman as a punishment (2 Kings 4:8-37, 2 Kings 5:20-27).

Achan took forbidden items from the city of Jericho after its conquest. This caused trouble for the Israelite people. When exposed, he and his family faced harsh consequences (Joshua 7:1-26).

In these stories, financial greed caused a lack of integrity. But there are other reasons people compromise their values.

Building integrity means always trying to do what's right, being honest, and treating others well. It's about learning, growing, and making the world a better place. Understanding and having integrity helps us make good choices and build trust with others.

Tips for building your integrity:
- Know Your Values: Understand what's important to you. These are the core principles that guide your choices.
- Think About Your Actions: Regularly think about the things you do. Ask yourself if they match with what you believe is right.

- Set High Standards: Aim to do the right thing, even when it's hard. Have strong rules for how you act.
- Tell the Truth: Always be honest. Don't make up stories or try to trick people.
- Keep Your Promises: Only say you'll do something if you're sure you can. If things change, talk about it and try to fix it.
- Say Sorry When You're Wrong: If you mess up, admit it. Saying sorry and trying to do better is important.
- Be Fair to Everyone: Treat everyone nicely, no matter who they are. Put yourself in their shoes.
- Do the Right Thing Every Time: Act the same way, whether others are watching or not.
- Show You Care: Understand how others feel. Be kind and show you care about them.
- Keep Trust: Make sure people can rely on you. Do what you say you will.
- Take Responsibility: If you make a mistake, own up to it. Fix what you can and learn from it.
- Ask for Advice: Talk to others and ask for their thoughts. Learn from what they say.
- Hang Out with Good People: Spend time with those who also care about doing the right thing.
- Make Your Own Rules: Write down what you think is right and wrong. Follow those rules.
- Learn All the Time: Keep learning about what's right and wrong. It helps you make good choices.

Discussion Questions: (Please limit to 4-5 questions that pertain to your group)

- How would you feel and handle it if you felt like you had to do something wrong to fit in with a group?
- In your opinion, why is it essential to make choices that align with your values, especially when you might face criticism from others?
- Can you think of a situation where doing the right thing was challenging but important?
- Think about someone you know with integrity and think about the amount of trust you have in that person. Do you think someone else is thinking of you when they answer that question?
- Why is having integrity important?
- Can you think of reasons other than wanting money that might make someone compromise their values?
- Can you share a time when someone's integrity made you trust them more?
- Can you think of any famous people who show a lot of integrity? What did they do to make you think they were people of integrity?
- What are some ways you can work on having more integrity in your own life?

Information for Instructors

Challenges:

- Some people may fear rejection or not fitting in with a particular group. The fear of rejection can cause individuals to conform to unethical behaviors or compromise their principles to gain acceptance.
- Some people fear confrontation or conflict and may compromise their integrity to avoid challenging situations. They might go along with unethical practices or decisions simply to maintain harmony or avoid rocking the boat.
- The fear of losing something valuable, such as a job, relationship, or status, can drive individuals to act in ways that compromise their integrity. This fear of loss may lead to unethical choices in an attempt to preserve what they have.
- The fear of being judged or criticized by others can influence individuals to engage in dishonest or deceitful behavior. They may act in ways that they believe will make them more acceptable to others, even if it means sacrificing their integrity.
- Individuals may compromise their integrity out of fear of the potential consequences of doing the right thing. This could include legal repercussions, financial losses, or damage to one's reputation. The fear of negative outcomes may lead to unethical decision-making.
- People who feel powerless or believe they have little control over their circumstances may be tempted to compromise their integrity as a way to gain some sense of control or influence.

Suggested Game: Two Truths and a Lie

Using three pieces of paper, write a large letter A, B, and C on each of the papers. Place the papers on a table lying in the center of the room. The audience will be on one side of the table, and the speaker will be on the opposite side. The first speaker will step behind the table, pick up the letter A, and make a statement. The speaker will move to the second and third papers, making a statement with each letter. One of the statements will be a lie. Only the participant will know which of the letters is the lie. The group will take turns guessing which statement is a lie.

You can track who manages to deceive the other players the most times. The ultimate winner is the one who can tell the most convincing lies, but everyone benefits from learning to recognize facial expressions and detect falsehoods.

NOTES:

CONFIDENCE
CHAPTER 5

DEFINITION

CONFIDENCE MEANS FEELING sure of yourself and your abilities. It's being cool and relaxed without feeling unsure or embarrassed. Confidence is also believing you can do something well and succeed at it. It's having faith in yourself and feeling ready to tackle life's challenges.

BIBLICAL REFERENCES

In the Bible, some stories show how having confidence in God can help in tough times. For example, David and Goliath (1 Samuel 17), Daniel in the Lions' Den (Daniel 6), Crossing the Red Sea (Exodus 14), and Shadrach, Meshach, and Abednego in the Fiery Furnace (Daniel 3).

These stories teach us about trust, faith, and having confidence in God's power and faithfulness. Even if the word "confidence" isn't used directly, the stories show relying on God with assurance in different difficult situations.

The Bible describes Christians in different ways that show their identity, purpose, and value. Here are some Bible verses that talk about this:

Chosen and Loved:

║ *Ephesians 1:4-5 (NIV): Talks about how God chose us to be special and loved.*

Children of God:

║ *John 1:12 (NIV): Says that if we believe in Jesus, we become God's children.*
║ *1 John 3:1 (NIV): Talks about how much God loves us and calls us His children.*

New Creation:

║ *2 Corinthians 5:17 (NIV): Says that if we follow Jesus, we become new people.*

A Royal Priesthood:

> *1 Peter 2:9 (NIV): Talks about how we're chosen, special, and belong to God.*

Citizens of Heaven:

> *Philippians 3:20 (NIV): Says that our real home is in heaven.*

Joint Heirs with Christ:

> *Romans 8:17 (NIV): Says that if we're God's children, we get to share in His good stuff.*

> *Ambassadors for Christ: 2 Corinthians 5:20 (NIV): Talks about how we represent Jesus here on earth.*

Set Apart and Holy:

1 Peter 1:15-16 (NIV): Says that because God is holy, we should try to be like Him.

These verses show that Christians are loved, chosen, transformed, and given a purpose by God. Knowing this can give Christians confidence and strength to face life's challenges. Everyone has a purpose and a reason for being on Earth. Sometimes, it's difficult to understand why you're here. Sometimes, you may feel like you don't belong. When you feel that, stop and remember you were created for a purpose. Be patient, and one day, you'll understand how much meaning your life has here on Earth.

Building confidence takes time and effort. Here are some tips to help you feel more confident:

- Set Realistic Goals: Break big goals into smaller ones that you can achieve.
- Celebrate Successes: Even small wins are worth celebrating.
- Think Positive: Replace negative thoughts with positive ones.
- Know Your Strengths: Focus on what you're good at.
- Embrace Challenges: See them as opportunities to learn and grow.
- Seek Support: Surround yourself with people who encourage you.
- Take Care of Yourself: Pay attention to your physical and mental health.
- Visualize Success: Imagine yourself succeeding in different situations.
- Learn from Mistakes: See them as chances to improve.
- Stay Persistent: Keep trying, even when things get tough.
- If you struggle with confidence, it's okay to ask for help from friends, family, or a professional. Remember, building confidence is a journey, so be patient with yourself and keep moving forward.

To gain confidence in yourself, you can work on understanding yourself better, thinking positively, setting realistic goals, getting support, and taking small steps to face your fears and challenges. Sometimes, getting help from a professional, such as a therapist or coach, can also be helpful.

Discussion Questions: (Please limit to 4-5 questions that pertain to your group)

- Why is it important to feel sure of yourself and your abilities?
- Talk about some stories from the Bible, like David and Goliath, Daniel in the Lions' Den, Crossing the Red Sea, and Shadrach, Meshach, and Abednego in the Fiery Furnace. How did confidence in God help the people in these stories face tough times?
- Even if the Bible doesn't use the word "confidence" directly, how do these stories still show the importance of trusting in God when things get hard?
- What do the Bible verses about Christians being loved, chosen, and having a purpose teach us? How can knowing these things give us confidence and strength?
- Why is it important to remember that everyone has a purpose in life, even when we feel like we don't fit in or we're not sure what our purpose is?
- How can having confidence in yourself and in God's plan help you when you're feeling unsure or insecure?
- Can you think of a time when feeling confident helped you do something well or overcome a problem?
- What are some ways we can build confidence in ourselves and our faith every day?
- Think about a time when you faced a challenge and felt unsure. How did you find the confidence to keep going? What did you learn from that experience?

INFORMATION FOR INSTRUCTORS

Challenges:

- Negative Self-Talk: Being too hard on yourself and having negative thoughts can make it hard to feel confident.
- Fear of Failure: Worrying about making mistakes or failing can stop you from feeling confident. It might also make you avoid trying new things.
- Comparison with Others: Constantly comparing yourself to others can make you feel like you're not good enough, which hurts your confidence.
- Lack of Skills or Knowledge: Feeling as if you don't know enough or aren't good at something can lower your confidence.
- Past Failures or Rejections: Bad experiences from the past can make you doubt yourself and your abilities.
- Perfectionism: Trying to be perfect in everything or you're never good enough.
- Lack of Positive Feedback: Not getting enough praise or encouragement from others can make it hard to feel confident.
- Social Anxiety: Feeling nervous in social situations or worrying about what others think can hurt your confidence.

- Physical Appearance Concerns: Feeling insecure about how you look can affect your confidence.
- Imposter Syndrome: Feeling like you're not as good as people think you are can make it hard to feel confident.

SUGGESTED GAME: POSITIVE AFFIRMATION BINGO

Positive affirmations can work wonders in cultivating a positive self-image. Create or download and print a customized Bingo game with squares containing uplifting affirmations such as "I am confident," "I embrace my uniqueness," and "I am worthy of love and happiness."

The online printable versions will also give you matching squares to call out bingo squares. As you draw the squares from a bowl or bag, the player matches the statement on their bingo card.

NOTES:

Helping Others Build Confidence
Chapter 6

Definition

L AST WEEK, YOU learned that confidence has different meanings, including a state of mind free of uncertainty, a belief in one's abilities, and a feeling of being able to succeed. This week's focus is on installing confidence in others. The Bible contains verses encouraging believers to uplift and encourage each other, even if the term "confidence" is not explicitly used. The underlying principles of promoting positivity and creating a supportive environment can be found throughout the Scriptures.

Biblical References

1 Thessalonians 5:11 (NIV):

> *"Therefore encourage one another and build each other up, just as in fact you are doing."*

Ephesians 4:29 (NIV):

> *"Do not let any unwholesome talk come out of your mouths, but only what is helpful for building others up according to their needs, that it may benefit those who listen."*

Proverbs 27:17 (NIV):

> *"As iron sharpens iron, so one person sharpens another."*

Hebrews 10:24-25 (NIV):

> *"And let us consider how we may spur one another on toward love and good deeds, not giving up meeting together, as some are in the habit of doing, but encouraging one another—and all the more as you see the Day approaching."*

Colossians 3:16 (NIV):

> *"Let the message of Christ dwell among you richly as you teach and admonish one another with all wisdom through psalms, hymns, and songs from the Spirit, singing to God with gratitude in your hearts."*

These verses remind us to communicate positively and support each other. Even though they don't use the word "confidence," they promote a positive and helpful community, which boosts confidence in individuals. Remember, building confidence takes time, and everyone's journey is different. Be there for others and help them along the way.

There are ways to encourage self-confidence in others:

- Help them replace negative thoughts with positive ones.
- Encourage them to focus on what they're good at.
- Tell them specific things you admire about them.
- Be honest and kind with your praise.
- Give feedback that helps them improve.
- Help them set goals they can reach.
- Celebrate their successes, no matter how small.
- Listen to their worries without judging them.
- Encourage them to try new things, even if it's scary.
- Remind them to take care of themselves.
- Show confidence in yourself too.
- Share stories of how you overcame challenges.
- Create a positive and supportive environment around you.
- Be patient and consistent in your support.

Discussion Questions: (Please limit to 4-5 questions that pertain to your group)

- What does it mean to "install confidence in others"?
- How can we help our friends or classmates feel more sure of themselves and their abilities?
- Can you think of a time when someone encouraged you and made you feel more confident?
- Even though the Bible verses don't use the word "confidence," how do they still teach us about helping each other feel good about ourselves?
- What does the saying "As iron sharpens iron, so one person sharpens another" from Proverbs 27:17 mean? Can you think of an example of how someone helped you improve or feel more confident?
- How does being around supportive people make us feel more confident?
- Why is it important to use kind and supportive words with each other, as the Bible says?
- How can our words either help or hurt someone's confidence?
- Sometimes it takes time to build confidence. How can we be patient with our friends as they learn to feel more sure of themselves?

- Can you think of ways we can encourage and support our friends or classmates to help them feel more confident?
- Think about a time when someone encouraged you and made you feel more confident. How did it make you feel, and how did it help you?
- How do you think we can create a positive and supportive environment in our school or community? What can you do to help make that happen?

INFORMATION FOR INSTRUCTORS

Challenges:

- Negative Self-talk: Being too hard on ourselves with negative thoughts can hurt our confidence.
- Fear of Failure: Being scared of making mistakes can stop us from feeling confident.
- Comparison with Others: Comparing ourselves to others can make us feel not good enough.
- Lack of Skills or Knowledge: Feeling as if we don't know enough can make us doubt ourselves.
- Past Failures or Rejections: Bad experiences from before can make us doubt ourselves.
- Perfectionism: Trying to be perfect can make us feel like we're never good enough.
- Lack of Positive Feedback: Not getting praise or encouragement can hurt our confidence.
- Social Anxiety: Being nervous around others can hurt our confidence, especially in social situations.
- Physical Appearance Concerns: Feeling bad about how we look can hurt our confidence.
- Imposter Syndrome: Feeling like we're not as good as people think can hurt our confidence.

SUGGESTED GAME: COMPLIMENT CHAIN

In a group setting, start a compliment chain where each person has to compliment the next. Reverse the chain and have everyone return compliments. Then, have all the participants change their seating positions and repeat the game. This fosters positivity and reminds your members of their worth.

NOTES:

Encouraging Others
Chapter 7

Definition

Encouraging others is to give courage, hope, confidence, and support. It can also be defined as the ability to inspire others. While the Bible may not explicitly focus on encouraging new ideas in the way we understand them today, several stories involve innovation, creativity, and thinking outside the box.

Biblical References

1 Thessalonians 5:11 (NIV):

> *"Therefore encourage one another and build each other up, just as in fact you are doing."*

Hebrews 10:24-25 (NIV):

> *"And let us consider how we may spur one another on toward love and good deeds, not giving up meeting together, as some are in the habit of doing, but encouraging one another—and all the more as you see the Day approaching."*

Ephesians 4:29 (NIV):

> *"Do not let any unwholesome talk come out of your mouths, but only what is helpful for building others up according to their needs, that it may benefit those who listen."*

Colossians 3:16 (NIV):

> *"Let the message of Christ dwell among you richly as you teach and admonish one another with all wisdom through psalms, hymns, and songs from the Spirit, singing to God with gratitude in your hearts."*

Romans 15:5 (NIV):

"May the God who gives endurance and encouragement give you the same attitude of mind toward each other that Christ Jesus had."

1 Corinthians 14:3 (NIV):

"But the one who prophesies speaks to people for their strengthening, encouraging and comfort."

2 Corinthians 1:3-4 (NIV):

"Praise be to the God and Father of our Lord Jesus Christ, the Father of compassion and the God of all comfort, who comforts us in all our troubles, so that we can comfort those in any trouble with the comfort we ourselves receive from God."

Proverbs 3:27 (NIV):

"Do not withhold good from those to whom it is due, when it is in your power to act."

To encourage someone, it helps to be empathetic, actively listen to others, and create an open and supportive environment where people feel comfortable sharing their thoughts and feelings. Encouragement doesn't always have to be grand gestures; sometimes, small acts of kindness and understanding can make a significant impact.

Tip on how to encourage others:

- Recognize and acknowledge their efforts and achievements, no matter how small. Genuine appreciation can go a long way in boosting someone's confidence.
- Instead of general compliments, be specific about what you appreciate. This shows that you are paying attention and genuinely value their contributions.
- When offering feedback, focus on constructive aspects. Highlight what they did well, and if there are areas for improvement, frame them in a positive and supportive manner.
- Show genuine interest in what others have to say. Listen actively, ask questions, and provide feedback that demonstrates your engagement and support.
- If someone is facing challenges, offer your assistance. Sometimes, knowing that others are willing to help can be a source of encouragement.
- Share stories of your challenges and successes. This can create a sense of connection and let others know that they are not alone in their struggles.
- Encourage others to set achievable goals. Unrealistic expectations can lead to frustration and disappointment. Help them break larger goals into smaller, more manageable tasks.
- Celebrate both small and significant achievements. Recognizing milestones, no matter how minor, reinforces positive behavior and motivates continued effort.

- Maintain a positive attitude, especially in challenging situations. Your optimism can be contagious and inspire others to approach difficulties with a constructive mindset.
- Let people know that you believe in their abilities. Your confidence in them can boost their self-esteem and encourage them to take on new challenges.
- Foster a supportive atmosphere where individuals feel comfortable expressing their ideas and taking risks without fear of harsh criticism.
- During tough times, provide emotional support. Let them know that setbacks are a part of the journey and you believe in their resilience.

Remember that everyone is motivated and encouraged in different ways, so it's essential to be attentive to individual needs and preferences. Being sincere, positive, and supportive can make a significant impact on others' confidence and motivation. Encouraging others is an important skill that can contribute to a positive and supportive environment.

Discussion Questions: (Please limit to 4-5 questions that pertain to your group)

- What does it mean to encourage someone?
- How does encouragement give people courage, hope, and confidence?
- Talk about the verses from the Bible, like 1 Thessalonians 5:11 and Hebrews 10:24-25. How do these verses encourage us to support and uplift each other?
- Can you think of a time when someone encouraged you and made you feel better?
- Even though the Bible doesn't talk about encouraging new ideas directly, how do you think encouraging others can still involve supporting innovation, creativity, and thinking outside the box?
- Why is it important to use kind and supportive words with each other, as Ephesians 4:29 says? How can our words help build others up and make them feel more confident?
- How do the verses in Colossians 3:16, Romans 15:5, and 1 Corinthians 14:3 show us the importance of encouraging and supporting each other? How does encouraging others reflect the attitude of Jesus?
- Proverbs 3:27 says, "Do not withhold good from those to whom it is due, when it is in your power to act." What does this mean? How can we use our abilities to encourage others?
- What are some ways we can encourage others?
- Can you think of examples of small acts of kindness that can make a big difference in someone's day?
- Why is it important to be empathetic and actively listen to others when we want to encourage them?
- How can creating an open and supportive environment help people feel comfortable sharing their thoughts and feelings?
- Think about a time when someone encouraged you or helped you through a tough situation. How did their support make you feel, and how did it impact you?
- What can you do to be more encouraging to those around you?

Information for Instructors

Challenges:

- Not Understanding Their Feelings: Sometimes, we might not fully understand what someone else is going through, making it hard to provide the right kind of encouragement.
- Fear of Saying the Wrong Thing: People might be afraid that they'll say something that could be taken the wrong way, so they hesitate to offer encouragement.
- Feeling Insecure Themselves: If someone is not feeling confident or secure in themselves, they might find it challenging to encourage others.
- Not Knowing How to Help: Some people genuinely want to help but may not know how, and that leads to feelings of helplessness.
- Cultural and Language Differences: Varied cultural backgrounds or language differences can create misunderstandings, making it difficult to provide effective encouragement.
- Busy Schedules: With hectic lifestyles, people may struggle to find time to support others, even if they want to.
- Fear of Rejection: The fear that their encouragement might be rejected or not appreciated can hold people back.
- Competition Among Peers: In competitive environments, individuals may be hesitant to encourage others due to concerns about rivalry.
- Not Recognizing the Need for Encouragement: Some people might not be aware of the struggles or challenges faced by others, making it difficult to offer support.
- Communication Challenges: Issues like poor communication skills or misunderstandings can hinder the effective expression of encouragement.

Suggested Game: The Encouragement Game

Sit in a circle and give everyone a piece of paper and a pen. Each person should write their name at the top of the piece of paper, then pass it to the person on their left. Each person then writes one or two (or more) positive characteristics about the person whose name is at the top of the paper. After 30-60 seconds, everyone passes the pieces of paper around to their left again. This continues until everyone has written on everyone else's paper. At the end of the game, everyone has the paper with their name at the top. Discuss what is written on the paper and how they feel about what others wrote about them.

NOTES:

ADAPTABILITY
CHAPTER 8

DEFINITION

Adaptability is the ability to adjust to different circumstances or conditions. It can also refer to the ability to change or be changed to fit new circumstances.

BIBLICAL REFERENCES

Joseph's life is a remarkable story of adaptability. He faced numerous challenges, from being sold into slavery by his brothers to being falsely accused and imprisoned. Despite these hardships, Joseph remained faithful and adaptable, using his God-given abilities to interpret dreams and eventually rising to a position of great authority in Egypt. His story highlights the importance of resilience and trust in God's plan, even when circumstances are difficult (Genesis 37-50).

The Book of Ruth tells the story of Ruth, a Moabite widow, and her mother-in-law, Naomi. Ruth's adaptability is evident as she leaves her homeland to accompany Naomi back to Israel. Ruth's loyalty, humility, and hard work eventually lead to her marriage with Boaz and becoming part of the lineage of King David. This story illustrates the rewards of adaptability and faithfulness (Book of Ruth).

The Apostle Paul's missionary journeys are marked by adaptability and resilience in the face of various challenges, such as opposition, persecution, and imprisonment. Paul faced adversity with a sense of purpose and flexibility, adjusting his approach based on the circumstances he encountered. His journeys, as documented in the Book of Acts, demonstrate the importance of adapting to different cultural contexts while remaining steadfast in spreading the message of Christ (The Book of Acts).

Adaptability is the ability to adjust to new conditions and changes in one's environment. While being adaptable is important, several things can make it difficult for a person to adapt.

Tips:

- Stay Positive: Keep a happy attitude, even when things get tough. Looking on the bright side can help you handle changes better.

- Learn New Things: Be curious and try to learn new stuff. Whether it's a new game, subject in school, or hobby, being open to learning makes it easier to adjust to different situations.
- Solve Problems: Get good at fixing issues. Think about solutions when things go wrong, and don't be afraid to ask for help when you need it.
- Be OK with Changes: Understand that things won't always stay the same. Embrace new situations instead of resisting them.
- Make Good Friends: Have friends who support you. It's easier to adapt to challenges when you have people who care about you.
- Listen to Feedback: When someone gives you advice, pay attention. Feedback helps you get better at things.
- Take Breaks: Sometimes, it's good to relax. Taking breaks helps you stay focused and deal with changes more easily.
- Think About Goals: Set small goals for yourself. Achieving them can boost your confidence and make you more adaptable.
- Don't Worry Too Much: Try not to stress about the future. Focus on what you can control and take things one step at a time.
- Be Flexible: Be open to changing your plans. It's okay if things don't go exactly how you expected.

To overcome barriers to being adaptable, people need to be aware of them and be willing to learn and try new things. Having a mindset that values flexibility and always trying to get better is important. Training programs, a supportive work culture, and good leaders can also help people and teams become more adaptable. Remember, everyone learns and grows at their own pace.

Discussion Questions: (Please limit to 4-5 questions that pertain to your group)

- Have you ever felt stuck or unable to try something new?
- Why do you think it's important for people to learn how to change and adapt?
- How can having a positive attitude help someone be better at dealing with new things?
- Can you think of a time when someone you know had to adjust to a big change? What did you do?
- Can you give examples of situations where someone might need to be adaptable?
- Let's talk about the stories of Joseph, Ruth, and the Apostle Paul from the Bible. How did each of them show adaptability when faced with challenges or changes?
- How did Joseph's ability to adapt help him rise to power in Egypt?
- Can you think of times when you had to adjust to unexpected changes in your own life?
- What can we learn from Ruth's story about the importance of being adaptable and faithful? How did her willingness to adapt lead to good things happening in her life?
- Why is it important to be adaptable in today's world?
- How can being adaptable help us deal with changes and challenges in school, at home, and in other parts of life?
- What are some things that might make it hard for someone to be adaptable?
- How can we learn to be more flexible and open to new things?

- Think about a time when you had to adapt to a new situation or place. How did you feel, and what did you do to adjust?
- How can we encourage each other to be more adaptable?
- What can we do to create a culture where being flexible and willing to change is valued?

INFORMATION FOR INSTRUCTORS

Challenges:

- Fear of Change: Some people are scared of change because they don't know what will happen or they're afraid of failing. This fear can stop them from trying new things.
- Lack of Open-mindedness: Some people are closed-minded, which means they have a hard time thinking about things in new ways. This makes it tough for them to adapt to different situations.
- Rigidity and Inflexibility: Some people are very set in their ways and don't like to change how they think or act. This can make it hard for them to adapt to new circumstances.
- Low Tolerance for Ambiguity: Some people don't like situations that are unclear or uncertain. They prefer things to be clear and definite, and this can make it hard for them to adapt when things are not so clear.
- Over-reliance on Past Success: If someone was successful doing something a certain way in the past, they might not want to try a different way, even if the situation has changed.
- Lack of Skills or Knowledge: If a person doesn't have the right skills or knowledge for a situation, they might find it hard to adapt. They might resist change because they feel like they don't know what to do.
- Organizational Culture: Some workplaces don't like to change, and this can make it tough for employees to adapt. People might be scared to suggest new ideas or take risks if they think they will get in trouble.
- Emotional Attachment: People can get very attached to the way things are done, and it can be hard for them to let go. This emotional connection can make it difficult for them to adapt to new practices.
- Lack of Support: If people don't feel supported by their friends, leaders, or the organization they work for, it can be hard for them to adapt. Support is important for helping people embrace change.
- Stress and Burnout: If someone is very stressed or burned out, they might not have the energy or ability to adapt. Stress can make it hard to think creatively or be open to change.

SUGGESTED GAME: "YES, AND"

Have your group sit in a circle or around a table. Tell participants that you are going to make up a conversation in which every sentence (except the first one) starts with the words "Yes, and…" First, demonstrate this yourself by making a simple statement. The next person will say "Yes, and.." and makes a statement that adds to the story. The game should continue around the circle or the table. In a fun game, every new statement will become more exaggerated and create some great stories. Go around the table or circle several times just to see how outrageous your story becomes.

NOTES:

Decision Making
Chapter 9

Definition

Decision-making is the process of choosing an option from several alternatives. It involves identifying a decision, gathering information, and assessing possible resolutions.

Biblical References

Moses faced a critical decision when he had to choose whether to identify with the Hebrews, his own people, or with the Egyptians, among whom he was raised. Ultimately, he chose to align himself with the Israelites and played a crucial role in leading them out of slavery (Exodus 2-4).

King Solomon, known for his wisdom, had to make a judgment concerning two women who claimed to be the mother of the same baby. His decision to suggest dividing the baby in half to test the women's reactions revealed the true mother's love and compassion (1 Kings 3:16-28).

The Prodigal Son tells the story of a young man who made the decision to ask for his inheritance early and then squandered it in a distant country. Later, he had to decide to return home and face his father, who, in turn, decided to forgive and welcome him back (Luke 15:11-32).

Daniel faced a decision regarding his diet while in Babylon. He chose not to defile himself with the king's food and wine, opting for a diet that adhered to his Jewish faith. This decision demonstrated Daniel's commitment to God's laws (Daniel 1:8).

These stories provide examples of individuals facing choices and making decisions following their faith, wisdom, or moral principles. They offer valuable insights into the importance of discernment, faithfulness, and the consequences of the choices we make. But, on the chance you make a bad decision, remember that God is always on the side of His children, and our worst mistakes can become His greatest glory.

Any barrier you may experience to good decision-making can be faced using the steps below:

1. Define the problem. What's the problem or opportunity you're facing?
2. Decide what you want to achieve with your choice. Make sure your goals are clear and achievable.

3. Collect facts and details that can help you understand the situation. Ask questions and find reliable sources.

4. Come up with different choices or ideas. Be creative and think about what could happen with each one.

5. Think about what's good and bad about each option. Consider what might happen if you choose one over the others.

6. Figure out what's most important to you. This could be cost, time, or other factors that matter in your decision.

7. Be ready to make decisions, even if they're not perfect. You might have to give up some things to get others.

8. Talk to people who know about the decision. Ask for their advice and listen to what they think.

9. Consider how you and others feel about the decision. Emotions are important, so pay attention to them.

10. Make your decision and put it into action. Follow through on what you decided to do.

11. After you see what happens, think about what you learned. What worked well, and what could you do better next time?

12. Reflect on your decisions from time to time. See how things are going and if you need to change anything.

13. Be flexible. If things change or you learn something new, be ready to adjust your decision.

Discussion Questions: (Please limit to 4-5 questions that pertain to your group)

- Have you ever had to decide between fitting in with one group or another?
- Have you ever had to make a tough choice that revealed something important about yourself?
- Have you ever had to make a decision that went against what everyone else was doing because of your beliefs?
- Have you ever had to forgive someone or been forgiven for your choice?
- How did Moses decide to help his people, the Israelites, instead of staying with the Egyptians? What do you think helped him make that decision?
- Why was King Solomon's decision about the baby so important? How did his wisdom help him figure out who the real mother was?
- According to the passage, which step or steps to making a good decision do you think is the most important?
- How do our feelings and emotions affect the decisions we make?
- Can you think of a time when your feelings influenced a decision you made?
- Why is it important to be willing to change our decisions if needed?
- Can you think of an example where being flexible led to a better outcome?
- Think about a decision you made recently. How did you go about making that decision, and what did you learn from it?

Information Information for Instructors

Challenges:

- Lack of Information: Sometimes, you might not have all the facts you need to make a good decision. It's like trying to solve a puzzle without all the pieces.
- Peer Pressure: Your friends might want you to do something, even if you think it's not the right choice. It's important to think for yourself and not just do what everyone else is doing.
- Emotions Taking Over: Strong feelings like anger, fear, or excitement can cloud your judgment. It's like a storm in your brain that makes it hard to see things clearly.
- Limited Experience: If you haven't been in a similar situation before, it's like trying to navigate a new place without a map. You might not know what to expect.
- Impulsivity: Making quick decisions without thinking about the consequences is like jumping into a pool without checking if there's water. Take a moment to consider what might happen next.
- Influence of Media: TV shows, movies, and social media can show things in a way that might not be real or healthy. It's important to be aware of what's true and what's just for entertainment.
- Fear of Failure: Sometimes, the fear of making a mistake or failing can hold you back from making a decision. It's okay to make mistakes; they help you learn and grow.
- Lack of Confidence: If you don't believe in yourself, it's like trying to ride a bike without knowing you can do it. Trust in your abilities and make choices that feel right for you.
- Not Considering Consequences: Forgetting to think about what might happen next is like setting off on a journey without packing essentials. Consider the pros and cons before deciding.
- Difficulty in Communication: If you find it hard to express your thoughts or listen to others, it's like trying to have a conversation in a language you don't understand. Work on communication skills to make better decisions together.

Suggested Game: Failure Fans

We're trying to create a new relationship to what we think of as failure. When we fail, it often means we're pushing ourselves to develop new skills. It means we're taking risks. Our so-called 'failures' can lead us to possibilities we never would have imagined. That's all worth celebrating.

Here, each person comes in front of the room one at a time and proudly shares a made-up failure. I am going to emphasize that the failures should be made up once the person gets to the stage. We don't want to initiate a therapy session here.

Once the made-up failure is shared, the rest of the group gives them wild and rousing applause. The person on stage should take a grand and deep "ta-da!" bow, soaking in the applause to full effect. The game finishes when everyone's had the chance to celebrate having 'failed.' Don't shrink from the applause; take a quick bow and run off stage. The whole point is to soak it in. What would it be like if we celebrated our failures?

So many of us remain terrified of failing or making mistakes, preventing us from even participating in discussions. This game builds a different relationship to failure.

NOTES:

EMPATHY
CHAPTER 10

DEFINITION

EMPATHY IS THE ability to understand another person's perspective, emotions, and experiences. It can also include the ability to share and respond to those experiences.

BIBLICAL REFERENCES

While the term "empathy" may not be explicitly mentioned in the Bible, there are biblical references and teachings that convey the importance of compassion, understanding, and caring for others. Here are a few biblical references related to empathy:

Galatians 6:2 (NIV):

> *"Carry each other's burdens, and in this way, you will fulfill the law of Christ."*

This verse shows us that we should help one another.

Philippians 2:4 (NIV):

> *"Not looking to your own interests but each of you to the interests of the others."*

This verse demonstrates that we should love others.

Colossians 3:12 (NIV):

> *"Therefore, as God's chosen people, holy and dearly loved, clothe yourselves with compassion, kindness, humility, gentleness, and patience."*

This verse demonstrates how we should treat other people. God says to treat others with compassion, kindness, humility, gentleness, and patience.

1 Peter 3:8 (NIV):

> *"Finally, all of you, be like-minded, be sympathetic, love one another, be compassionate and humble."*

Matthew 7:12 (NIV):

> *"So in everything, do to others what you would have them do to you, for this sums up the Law and the Prophets."*

While these verses may not explicitly use the word "empathy," they emphasize the principles of understanding, compassion, and putting oneself in the shoes of others. The Bible encourages believers to treat others with kindness and to be aware of the feelings and struggles of those around them.

Tips on being more empathetic:

- Actively Listen: When someone talks to you, really listen. Nodding, making eye contact, and appropriately responding show them that you care about what they're saying.
- Imagine Their Feelings: Try to put yourself in their shoes. Think about how they might be feeling in a particular situation. This helps you understand and connect with their emotions.
- Ask Questions: Encourage others to share by asking open-ended questions. These are questions that can't be answered with just a "yes" or "no," and they help deepen conversations.
- Avoid Judging: Don't be quick to judge others. Everyone has their own unique experiences, so try to understand their perspective without making assumptions.
- Read Stories: Explore books or stories that tell different tales and perspectives. This can help you see the world through others' eyes, making you more empathetic.
- Help Others: Volunteer or do kind things for people. This exposes you to different situations and people, fostering a sense of compassion.
- Say Thank You: Express gratitude for the positive aspects of your relationships. Being thankful helps you connect with others on an emotional level.
- Understand Your Emotions: Reflect on your personal feelings and how they might influence your thoughts. This self-awareness makes it easier to relate to others.
- Communicate Empathetically: Be careful with your words, considering how they might affect others. Use "I" statements to express your feelings, creating a supportive environment.

It's important to understand and work on these things to create a kind and caring environment. This means knowing yourself, being ready to learn, and trying to break down these barriers for better connections with others. Remember, becoming more empathetic takes time. Be genuinely interested, patient, and willing to understand others. By trying these tips, you can grow your empathy and build stronger connections with those around you.

Discussion Questions: (Please limit to 4-5 questions that pertain to your group)

- Why do you think understanding, stereotypes, fear, and other things can stop us from connecting emotionally with others?

- Have you ever been in a situation where you didn't quite understand how someone felt? How did that make you feel, and what could have helped you understand better?
- Do you think cultural rules or societal expectations can affect how much we show we care?
- How can we challenge cultural or societal expectations to create a more caring environment?
- Can you give an example of a time when you understood how someone else felt?
- Even though the Bible doesn't use the word "empathy," how do the verses listed demonstrate why understanding and caring about others is important.
- What does Galatians 6:2 mean when it says we should "carry each other's burdens"?
- How does helping each other make a difference in our lives?
- How does Philippians 2:4 encourage us to think about other people's needs, not just our own?
- Can you think of a time when you did something nice for someone else?
- What does Colossians 3:12 teach us about how to treat other people?
- Why is it important to be kind and patient with others?
- In 1 Peter 3:8, it says we should be sympathetic and compassionate toward others. Can you think of a time when someone was compassionate toward you?
- How can knowing ourselves, being open to learning, and breaking down barriers help us understand others better, as mentioned in the passage?
- Why is it important to be patient and willing to understand others when we're trying to be more empathetic?
- Can you think of a time when someone listened to you and understood how you felt?
- How do you think being empathetic can help us make friends and create a nicer environment at school or in our community?
- What can you do to show empathy to others?

INFORMATION FOR INSTRUCTORS

Challenges:

Being understanding and caring about others is important, but sometimes, it's hard for people to show their feelings. Here are some reasons:

- Understanding: Sometimes, not understanding how others feel can make it tough to be caring. It's important to try to see things from different points of view to care about someone truly.
- Stereotypes: Judging people based on ideas we already have in our minds can stop us from really caring. Understanding each person for who they are is better than relying on preconceived notions.
- Fear: People might avoid being caring because they're afraid of being open and vulnerable. They worry that showing they care could make them feel too exposed or that others might use it against them.
- Cultural Differences: Differences in where people come from, how much money they have,

or what they've been through can make it hard to connect. Not being aware of these differences can stop us from understanding others emotionally.

- Personal Problems: When someone is dealing with personal issues, it's tough for them to think about and care for others. Personal problems can make it hard to show that we care about someone else's struggles.

- Communication: If someone is not good at talking or doesn't communicate well, it can be a barrier to understanding and showing empathy. Misunderstandings can happen, making it hard to connect emotionally.

- Feeling in the Head, Not the Heart: Some people find it hard to turn their understanding of someone else's feelings into a real emotional connection. This difference between knowing and feeling can create a barrier to empathy.

- Feeling Tired Emotionally: Always dealing with others' emotions without taking care of our own can lead to feeling emotionally tired. This tiredness can make it tough to consistently show that we care.

- Having Ways to Cope: Some people have developed ways to deal with things that involve keeping their emotions at a distance. This can stop them from making emotional connections with others.

- Following Cultural Rules: In some cultures or places, some rules say people shouldn't show too much emotion or vulnerability. This makes it hard for individuals to openly show that they care about others.

SUGGESTED GAME: EMOTIONAL CHARADES

Emotional Charades is played in the traditional sense, but this time, emotions are whispered to individuals acting out their emotions. Here is a list:

1. Happiness	11. Embarrassment	21. Nervousness
2. Sadness	12. Envy	22. Amusement
3. Anger	13. Jealousy	23. Gratitude
4. Fear	14. Frustration	24. Compassion
5. Surprise	15. Contentment	25. Sympathy
6. Disgust	16. Relief	26. Boredom
7. Excitement	17. Guilt	27. Curiosity
8. Anxiety	18. Shame	28. Anticipation
9. Love	19. Pride	29. Regret
10. Confusion	20. Loneliness	30. Hope

Notes:

RESILIENCY
CHAPTER 11

DEFINITION

RESILIENCY MEANS BEING able to bounce back when things get tough. It's about being strong and flexible enough to handle challenges without giving up. Resilient people can adapt to difficult situations and find ways to overcome them. They have supportive friends and family and know how to stay positive even when times are hard. Resilience is like a muscle you can strengthen over time by learning how to solve problems, staying connected with others, and staying hopeful.

BIBLICAL REFERENCES

In the Bible, several passages touch upon the theme of resilience and perseverance in the face of adversity. Here are a few:

James 1:2-4 (NIV):

> *"Consider it pure joy, my brothers and sisters, whenever you face trials of many kinds, because you know that the testing of your faith produces perseverance. Let perseverance finish its work so that you may be mature and complete, not lacking anything."*

Romans 5:3-4 (NIV):

> *"Not only so, but we also glory in our sufferings, because we know that suffering produces perseverance; perseverance, character; and character, hope."*

Hebrews 10:35-36 (NIV):

> *"So do not throw away your confidence; it will be richly rewarded. You need to persevere so that when you have done the will of God, you will receive what he has promised."*

These verses emphasize the importance of enduring trials with patience and faith, trusting that perseverance leads to growth, maturity, and eventual reward. They offer encouragement to remain steadfast in the face of challenges, knowing that there is purpose and hope in difficult times. And lastly, remember the words of Charles Spurgeon, "By perseverance, the snail reached the ark."

Here are some tips for building resiliency:

- Stay Connected: Spend time with family and friends who support you. Talking to them about your feelings can help you feel better during tough times.
- Think Positive: Try to focus on the good things in life, even when things are hard. Believe in yourself and your ability to get through challenges.
- Learn to Solve Problems: When something goes wrong, try to think of solutions instead of feeling overwhelmed. Break big problems into smaller ones and tackle them one step at a time.
- Take Care of Yourself: Eat healthy foods, get enough sleep, and exercise regularly. Taking care of your body can help you handle stress better.
- Stay Flexible: Be open to change and willing to adapt when things don't go as planned. Being flexible can help you bounce back from setbacks more easily.
- Find Activities You Enjoy: Doing things you love, like hobbies or sports, can boost your mood and help you relax when you're feeling stressed.
- Help Others: Volunteering or helping out friends and family can make you feel good about yourself and strengthen your relationships.
- Ask for Help When You Need It: Don't be afraid to reach out to trusted adults, like parents, teachers, or school counselors, if you're struggling. They're there to support you.

Discussion Questions: (Please limit to 4-5 questions that pertain to your group)

- Can you think of a time when you or someone you know showed resilience?
- Thinking about the things that can get in the way of being resilient, like not having enough support or feeling alone, which ones do you think affect people the most?
- Do you have any personal stories or strategies for staying strong during tough times that you'd like to share with the group?
- What do you think the quote, "By perseverance, the snail reached the ark," means concerning resilience?
- Even though the Bible doesn't say "resilience," how do the verses from James, Romans, and Hebrews show us why it's important to stay strong when things are hard?
- Discuss James 1:2-4. Why does it say we should think of trials as a good thing? How can challenges help us grow and become better people?
- How does Romans 5:3-4 encourage us to think about tough times differently? What does it say suffering can lead to, and why is that important?
- In Hebrews 10:35-36, why are we encouraged not to give up? What does it mean to persevere and do what God wants us to do?
- How can solving problems, staying connected with others, and staying hopeful help us become more resilient as it says in the definition?

- Why is it important to have supportive friends and family when things are tough?
- Can you think of a time when someone's support helped you get through a hard time?
- What are some ways we can get better at being resilient, like working a muscle?
- Can you think of any ways you stay positive when things are tough?

INFORMATION FOR INSTRUCTORS

Barriers to resiliency can vary depending on individual circumstances, but some common barriers include:

- Support: If you don't have people like family, friends, or a community to help you when things are tough, it can make it harder to stay strong. It's really important to have people who care about you.
- Thinking negatively: If you often think negatively, like always expecting the worst or doubting yourself, it can be harder to handle tough situations.
- Not Knowing How to Handle Problems: If you're not good at dealing with problems or tough times, it can feel overwhelming and like you're stuck.
- History: If you've been through really tough times or bad experiences before, it can make it harder to deal with new challenges.
- Feeling Sick: If you're not feeling well physically, it can make it harder to handle stress or tough situations.
- Not Having Enough Money: If you're always worried about money or don't have enough, it can add a lot of stress and make it harder to stay strong.
- Feeling Alone: If you feel like you're all by yourself and don't have anyone to talk to or help you out, it can make tough situations even harder.
- Not Knowing How to Change Things: If you're not good at figuring out how to solve problems or make things better when they're tough, it can feel like you're stuck and can't get through it.

SUGGESTED GAME: SOUND EFFECTS

In this game, two players act out a scene, but two additional players provide the sound effects. This is great for communication and creativity! It's also a great way to include your shy participants, as making sounds isn't as intimidating as coming up with dialogue. Improv games encourage creativity, adaptability, and quick thinking, all of which are important aspects of resilience.

NOTES:

ACCOUNTABILITY
CHAPTER 12

DEFINITION

Accountability means being responsible for what you do and the choices you make. It's about owning up to your actions and the results that come from them. When you're accountable, you're honest about what you've done, even if it's a mistake. You're willing to admit when you've messed up and take steps to fix it. Accountability is important because it helps build trust, shows that you're reliable, and encourages you to do the right thing. Whether it's in school, at home, or with friends, being accountable means being someone others can count on.

BIBLICAL REFERENCES

Romans 14:12 (NIV):

> *"So then, each of us will give an account of ourselves to God."*

This verse emphasizes the individual responsibility each person has before God and the ultimate accountability to Him.

Galatians 6:5 (NIV):

> *"For each one should carry their own load."*

Here, individuals are reminded of their responsibility to bear their own burdens and be accountable for their actions.

Matthew 12:36 (NIV):

> *"But I tell you that everyone will have to give account on the day of judgment for every empty word they have spoken."*

This verse highlights the idea that even our words will be subject to judgment and accountability before God.

Luke 12:48b (NIV):

> *"From everyone who has been given much, much will be demanded; and from the one who has been entrusted with much, much more will be asked."*

This verse underscores the principle of accountability based on the resources, opportunities, and abilities entrusted to each individual.

James 4:17 (NIV):

> *"If anyone, then, knows the good they ought to do and doesn't do it, it is sin for them."*

This verse emphasizes the accountability that comes with knowing what is right and failing to act accordingly.

These verses, among others in the Bible, show the importance of accountability before God and in our relationships with others. They emphasize the need for individuals to take responsibility for their actions and to be mindful of their obligations to God and their fellow human beings.

Here are some tips on gaining accountability:

- Own up to mistakes: When you make a mistake, admit it instead of trying to hide or blame others. It shows you're responsible.
- Understand your responsibilities: Make sure you know what you're supposed to do so you can do it well.
- Think about consequences: Before you act, think about what might happen if you don't do what you're supposed to. It can help you make better choices.
- Ask for help: If you're not sure what to do, it's okay to ask for help. It's better to ask than to do something wrong.
- Set goals: Decide what you want to accomplish and make a plan to get there. It helps you stay focused and accountable.
- Keep track of your progress: Write down what you've done and what you still need to do. It helps you stay organized and accountable.
- Be honest: Always tell the truth, even if it's hard. People will trust you more if they know they can rely on you.
- Learn from mistakes: When things don't go as planned, think about what you can do differently next time. It helps you grow and become more accountable.
- Stay motivated: Remember why being accountable is important to you. It can help you stay focused and committed.
- Celebrate successes: When you meet your goals or do something well, celebrate! It keeps you motivated and encourages you to continue being accountable.

Discussion Questions: (Please limit to 4-5 questions that pertain to your group)

- Do you think being accountable gets easier or harder as you grow older? Why?

- Can you give an example of a time when you took responsibility for something you did, whether it was good or bad?
- Even though the Bible doesn't use the word "accountability," how do the verses from Romans, Galatians, Matthew, Luke, and James show us why it's important to be responsible for our actions?
- How does Galatians 6:5 remind us of our responsibility to carry our own load?
- Why is it important to be accountable for our actions and not rely on others to fix our mistakes?
- Reflect on Luke 12:48b. What does it mean to you when it says "much will be demanded" from those who have been given much? How can this verse inspire us to use our abilities and resources wisely?
- Discuss James 4:17. Why is it considered a sin if we know what is right but choose not to do it? How does this verse challenge us to take responsibility for our actions?
- Why is it important to be someone others can count on, as mentioned in the passage?
- Can you think of a time when someone's accountability made a positive impact on you or your community?
- What are some ways we can practice accountability in our daily lives, whether it's at school, at home, or with friends?
- Can you think of any personal strategies for owning up to our actions and making things right when we make mistakes?
- How can the lessons from the Bible about accountability help us become better people and build stronger relationships with others?

INFORMATION FOR INSTRUCTORS

Being accountable can be challenging due to various Challenges:

- Being afraid of getting in trouble: Some people don't want to be accountable because they're afraid of getting yelled at or punished.
- Not understanding what to do: Sometimes, people don't know exactly what they're supposed to be responsible for, so they avoid taking charge.
- Blaming others: Instead of admitting when they've done something wrong, some people blame someone else or say it's not their fault.
- Being too proud: People with big egos find it hard to admit they've made a mistake or aren't perfect.
- Not trusting others: When people don't trust the people around them, they don't want to be responsible for anything because they're worried they'll be treated unfairly.
- Not talking clearly: If instructions or expectations aren't explained well, it's tough for people to know what they're supposed to do.
- Thinking things aren't fair: If people feel like they're being treated unfairly, they don't want to be responsible for anything.

- Having too much to do: When people have a lot of work or stress, they might forget or not have time to be accountable.
- Not facing the consequences: If nothing happens when people don't do what they're supposed to, they won't feel like they need to be responsible.
- Following what others do: Sometimes, people don't want to be accountable because everyone else isn't being responsible either.

SUGGESTED GAME: THE BLINDFOLDED OBSTACLE COURSE

A blindfolded obstacle course is a game where one person wears a blindfold, and the other person guides them through an obstacle course using only their voice. I love this game because it inspires so many other characteristics, such as trust, focus, and listening skills.

NOTES:

Strategic Thinking
Chapter 13

Definition

STRATEGIC THINKING MEANS planning and making smart decisions to reach your goals. It's like playing chess, where you think about your moves and what your opponent might do next. It involves considering different options and choosing the best ones to get where you want to go. Strategic thinking helps you solve problems effectively and be successful in whatever you're trying to achieve.

Biblical References

While the term "strategic thinking" may not be explicitly mentioned in the Bible, there are many passages that emphasize the importance of wisdom, planning, and foresight, which are key elements of strategic thinking. Here are a few biblical references that relate to strategic thinking:

Proverbs 15:22 (NIV):

"*Plans fail for lack of counsel, but with many advisers they succeed.*"

This verse highlights the importance of seeking advice and counsel from others when making decisions, which is a key aspect of strategic thinking.

Proverbs 16:3 (NIV):

"*Commit to the Lord whatever you do, and he will establish your plans.*"

This verse encourages individuals to seek guidance from God in their planning and decision-making processes, trusting that He will lead them in the right direction.

Proverbs 21:5 (NIV):

"*The plans of the diligent lead to profit as surely as haste leads to poverty.*"

This verse underscores the importance of careful planning and hard work in achieving success, which are essential components of strategic thinking.

Luke 14:28-30 (NIV):

> *"Suppose one of you wants to build a tower. Won't you first sit down and estimate the cost to see if you have enough money to complete it? For if you lay the foundation and are not able to finish it, everyone who sees it will ridicule you, saying, 'This person began to build and wasn't able to finish.'"*

This passage from the New Testament emphasizes the importance of counting the cost and planning before undertaking any endeavor, which is a key aspect of strategic thinking.

These biblical references illustrate the importance of wisdom, planning, and seeking guidance from God in making decisions and pursuing goals, all of which are fundamental aspects of strategic thinking.

By recognizing and overcoming the barriers of strategic thinking, you can improve your strategic thinking and make better decisions in various aspects of your life. By incorporating these tips into your daily life and decision-making processes, you can enhance your strategic thinking abilities and become more effective in achieving your goals.

Here are some tips to develop strategic thinking:

- Set Clear Goals: Identify what you want to achieve in the short-term and long-term. Having clear goals will give you direction and focus your strategic thinking efforts.
- Gather Information: Take the time to gather relevant information about the situation you're facing. This includes understanding the context, identifying key stakeholders, and gathering data that will inform your decisions.
- Think Critically: Practice questioning assumptions and evaluating information critically. Look for patterns, connections, and potential consequences of different actions.
- Consider Alternatives: Don't settle for the first solution that comes to mind. Instead, brainstorm multiple alternatives and evaluate their pros and cons before making a decision.
- Seek Input from Others: Don't be afraid to ask for input from colleagues, mentors, or experts in the field. Different perspectives can help you see things from angles you may not have considered.
- Anticipate Challenges: Take time to think about potential obstacles or challenges that may arise along the way. Develop contingency plans to address these challenges and keep your strategic thinking flexible.
- Learn from Experience: Reflect on past experiences and learn from both successes and failures. This will help you refine your strategic thinking skills over time.
- Stay Open-Minded: Be open to new ideas and feedback. Avoid being too rigid in your thinking and be willing to adapt your strategies based on new information or changing circumstances.
- Practice Decision-Making: Actively practice making decisions, even if they are small ones. This will help you build confidence in your ability to think strategically and make sound judgments.

- Stay Persistent: Developing strategic thinking takes time and practice. Don't get discouraged by setbacks, and keep working on honing your skills over time.

Discussion Questions: (Please limit to 4-5 questions that pertain to your group)

- Can you give an example of strategic thinking from your own life or something you've seen in movies or books?
- Why is it important to consider different options and plan ahead before making decisions?
- Do you agree that seeking advice, trusting in guidance, and careful planning are important aspects of making smart decisions? Why or why not?
- Can you think of a time when someone else's perspective helped you see things differently?
- Think about your life goal. Can you break that goal into small tasks that you can accomplish daily to achieve that goal?
- Can you give an example of a time when you had to plan ahead to reach a goal?
- Even though the Bible doesn't say "strategic thinking," how do the verses from Proverbs and Luke show us why it's important to think carefully before making decisions?
- Let's talk about Proverbs 15:22. Why do you think it says plans fail without counsel? How can talking to others help us make better decisions?
- Reflect on Proverbs 21:5. What does it mean when it says diligent planning leads to success?
- How can planning and hard work help us achieve our goals?
- Discuss Luke 14:28-30. Why is it important to think about the cost before starting something? How can this relate to our everyday choices?
- What are some ways we can practice strategic thinking every day?
- Can you share any tips for making smart decisions and reaching our goals?
- How do the lessons from the Bible about planning and seeking guidance inspire us to become better thinkers and achieve success?
- What can we learn from these verses about the importance of thinking ahead and trusting in God's plan for us?

Information for Instructors

Barriers to strategic thinking:

- Lack of Information: If you don't have all the facts or don't understand the situation fully, it's like trying to solve a puzzle without all the pieces. This can make it hard to make smart decisions.
- Narrow-mindedness: Sometimes, people only consider one way of doing things or one point of view. This limits their ability to see other possibilities and come up with creative solutions.
- Fear of Failure: Being afraid to make mistakes can hold you back from trying new things or taking risks. But making mistakes is a part of learning and growing.

- Relying on Habit: Doing things the same way just because it's how they've always been done can prevent you from exploring better ways of doing things.
- Overconfidence: Thinking you have all the answers and not being open to input from others can blind you to potential problems or better solutions.
- Lack of Patience: Strategic thinking often requires taking time to analyze situations and consider different options. Rushing through decisions can lead to poor choices.
- Resistance to Change: Some people are uncomfortable with change and prefer to stick with what's familiar, even if it's not the best option for the future.

Suggested Game: Chess

Chess is a classic strategy game that requires players to think several moves ahead, anticipate their opponent's moves, and adapt their strategy accordingly. It's a great way to develop strategic thinking and problem-solving skills. You may have to teach the participants how to play.

*Many online video games that teens play daily teach strategic thinking skills.

NOTES:

DELEGATION
CHAPTER 14

DEFINITION

DELEGATING IS WHEN you give someone else the authority to do something for you. It's like asking a friend to water your plants while you're on vacation or letting a teammate handle part of a group project. Instead of doing everything yourself, you trust someone else to help out.

BIBLICAL REFERENCES

In the Bible, several passages touch upon the concept of delegating work or entrusting tasks to others.

Exodus 18:13-27: This passage describes how Moses, upon the advice of his father-in-law Jethro, delegates the responsibility of judging disputes among the Israelites to capable leaders. Jethro advises Moses to appoint trustworthy individuals to assist him in handling the workload, thereby lightening his own burden.

Matthew 25:14-30 (Parable of the Talents): In this parable, Jesus tells the story of a master who entrusts varying amounts of money (talents) to his servants before going away on a journey. The servants are expected to invest and manage the talents wisely during their master's absence. This parable illustrates the importance of faithful stewardship and effective delegation of resources.

Acts 6:1-7: This passage recounts the early Christian community facing a problem related to the distribution of food to widows. The apostles decide to delegate this responsibility to others, selecting seven men full of faith and the Holy Spirit to oversee the task. By delegating this duty, the apostles were able to focus on their primary responsibilities of preaching and prayer.

The biblical references emphasize the principles of wise delegation, recognizing the need to share responsibilities and empower others to contribute to the community's well-being. If you need to delegate work, please remember to ask nicely. Nicely delegating work involves clear communication and respect for others' abilities and time.

Here are some steps to delegate work in a friendly and effective manner:

1. Choose the Right Person: Select someone who has the skills and capabilities to successfully complete the task. Consider their workload and availability as well.
2. Explain the Task: Clearly outline what needs to be done, including specific instructions, goals, and deadlines. Provide any necessary resources or support to help them succeed.
3. Show Confidence: Express your confidence in the person's ability to handle the task. Let them know why you're delegating to them and how it fits into the bigger picture.
4. Be Open to Questions: Encourage the person to ask questions if they're unsure about anything. Offer guidance and clarification as needed to ensure they understand what's expected.
5. Offer Support: Let them know you're available to provide assistance or guidance if they encounter any challenges along the way. Make it clear that you're there to help them succeed.
6. Provide Feedback: Once the task is completed, offer constructive feedback on their performance. Recognize their efforts and achievements, and provide guidance for improvement if necessary.
7. Say Thank You: Show appreciation for their efforts and willingness to take on the task. A simple thank you goes a long way in making the person feel valued and respected.

By following these steps, you can delegate work in a way that is both kind and effective, fostering a positive working relationship and promoting success.

Discussion Questions: (Please limit to 4-5 questions that pertain to your group)

- Can you give an example of when you asked someone to help you with something?
- In the story of Moses from the Bible, why did he need to ask others for help with judging disputes among the Israelites?
- Can you explain the Parable of the Talents from the Bible? How does it teach us about using our skills wisely and trusting others with responsibilities?
- Why did the apostles in the Bible delegate the task of distributing food to widows? How did this help them focus on their main jobs?
- Why is it important to ask for help in a kind and respectful way, as mentioned in the passage?
- How can clear communication and respecting others' abilities make asking for help better?
- What are some suggested steps for asking someone for help with a task? Why is each step important?
- Can you tell about a time when you asked someone for help? How did you choose the right person, and what did you do to make sure they understood what to do?
- How does offering support and feedback help the person you're asking for help?
- Why is it important to say thank you?
- What are some good things about asking for help instead of doing everything yourself?
- Can you think of a time when asking for help might not be the best choice?
- How can we use what we learned about asking for help in our everyday lives?

- What are some tasks you could ask others to help you with to make things easier?

INFORMATION FOR INSTRUCTORS

Barriers to delegating work:

- Perfectionism: Sometimes people don't want to share tasks because they worry they won't be done perfectly. They think they're the only ones who can do it right.
- Lack of Trust: If you don't trust others to do a good job, you might not want to give them tasks. You worry they might mess things up.
- Micromanagement Tendencies: Some people want to control every little detail. They have trouble letting others do things on their own.
- Time Constraints: When you're busy, it seems easier to do things yourself than explain them to others. But in the long run, it's better to share tasks.
- Fear of Losing Authority or Recognition: People might worry that if they give tasks to others, they'll seem less important. They want to be seen as the ones who get things done.
- Lack of Communication Skills: Sometimes, people have trouble explaining what they need from others. This makes it hard to share tasks effectively.
- Overloaded Team Members: If everyone is already swamped with work, leaders might hesitate to give them even more. They don't want to make things too hard for their team.

SUGGESTED GAME: SCAVENGER HUNT

Scavenger hunts are a fun way to get teams working together and can help teach delegation, problem-solving, planning, and strategy. Forming a group and declaring a leader to delegate the products to search for is a great way to teach individuals how to delegate.

NOTES:

EMPOWERMENT
CHAPTER 15

DEFINITION

EMPOWERMENT MEANS GIVING people the ability to take control of their own lives and make decisions for themselves. It's about providing them with the tools, skills, and knowledge they need to solve problems and achieve their goals. When someone is empowered, they feel confident and independent, and they can stand up for themselves and others. Empowerment is important because it helps individuals and communities overcome challenges and create positive change in society.

BIBLICAL REFERENCES

The Bible contains several passages that can be interpreted as references to empowerment.

Philippians 4:13 (NIV):

> *"I can do all this through him who gives me strength."*

This verse suggests that believers can accomplish anything through their faith in God, implying a sense of empowerment derived from spiritual strength.

Isaiah 40:29 (NIV):

> *"He gives strength to the weary and increases the power of the weak."*

Here, it is emphasized that God provides strength and power to those who are weak or weary, implying empowerment through divine assistance.

2 Timothy 1:7 (NIV):

> *"For the Spirit God gave us does not make us timid, but gives us power, love and self-discipline."*

This verse suggests that believers are endowed with power, love, and self-discipline through the Holy Spirit, indicating a sense of empowerment through faith.

Luke 10:19 (NIV):

> *"I have given you authority to trample on snakes and scorpions and to overcome all the power of the enemy; nothing will harm you."*

In this passage, Jesus empowers his disciples with authority over evil forces, indicating a form of empowerment granted by divine authority.

Ephesians 3:16 (NIV):

> *"I pray that out of his glorious riches he may strengthen you with power through his Spirit in your inner being."*

This verse highlights the role of God's Spirit in strengthening believers with power within themselves, implying a form of inner empowerment.

These verses are often interpreted to convey the idea that believers are empowered by their faith and connection with God to overcome challenges, achieve their goals, and live fulfilling lives.

Becoming more empowered means feeling stronger and more in control of your own life. Here are some ways to do that:

- Believe in Yourself: Start by believing in yourself and your abilities. Trust that you can handle whatever comes your way.
- Set Goals: Decide what you want to achieve and set goals for yourself. Break them down into smaller steps to make them more manageable.
- Learn New Things: Keep learning and expanding your knowledge. Education gives you the power to understand the world better and make informed decisions.
- Speak Up: Don't be afraid to speak up for yourself and others. Your voice matters, and speaking out can help bring about positive changes.
- Build Relationships: Surround yourself with supportive people who lift you up and encourage you to be the best version of yourself.
- Take Care of Yourself: Make sure to take care of your physical and mental health. When you feel good physically and mentally, you're better able to face challenges.
- Stand Up for What's Right: Stand up against injustice and unfairness, even if it's difficult. Being empowered means fighting for what's right.
- Practice Resilience: Understand that setbacks are a natural part of life. Learn from them, pick yourself up, and keep moving forward.
- Help Others: Empowerment isn't just about yourself; it's also about lifting others up. Offer support and encouragement to those around you.
- Stay Positive: Stay positive and focus on the things you can control. A positive mindset can help you overcome obstacles and achieve your goals.

Discussion Questions: (Please limit to 4-5 questions that pertain to your group)

- What does empowerment mean to you based on the definition provided?

- Can you think of examples from your own life or the lives of others that illustrate empowerment?
- How can we support each other in overcoming barriers to empowerment and promoting a culture of empowerment in our communities?
- Do you think any additional barriers to empowerment were not mentioned?
- Think about a time when you felt empowered. What factors contributed to that feeling?
- Can you think of a time when someone being empowered helped them overcome a challenge?
- What are some ways to become more empowered?
- Which way of becoming more empowered do you think is the most helpful, and why?
- How does believing in yourself make you feel more empowered?
- Can you tell a story about a time when believing in yourself helped you achieve something?
- Why is it a good idea to set goals for yourself?
- How does learning new things help you become more empowered?
- Can you give an example of how learning something new made you feel more confident?
- Why is it important to speak up for yourself and others?
- Can you tell a story about a time when someone's support helped you feel stronger?
- Why is it important to take care of your physical and mental health to feel empowered?
- Can you think of ways to take care of yourself both physically and mentally?

Information for Instructors

Barriers to becoming empowered:

- Limited access to education: When people don't have the opportunity to learn important skills or gain knowledge, it becomes difficult for them to make informed decisions and take charge of their lives effectively.
- Economic disparities: Financial struggles and inequalities can hinder individuals from accessing resources, opportunities, and support systems necessary for empowerment. This lack of financial stability can limit their ability to pursue their goals and aspirations.
- Social and cultural constraints: Traditional societal norms and cultural expectations may impose restrictions on certain groups, such as women or minorities, preventing them from fully participating in decision-making processes or asserting their rights.
- Prejudice and discrimination: Discriminatory attitudes and practices based on factors like race, gender, sexuality, or disability can undermine individuals' confidence and limit their opportunities for empowerment, making them feel marginalized and excluded.
- Limited political participation: A lack of access to political processes, such as voting rights or representation in government, can prevent individuals from influencing policies that affect their lives, thereby diminishing their sense of agency and empowerment.
- Power imbalances: Unequal distribution of power within relationships, institutions, or

society can create barriers to empowerment by limiting individuals' ability to advocate for themselves, challenge oppressive structures, or access opportunities on an equal basis.

- Psychological Challenges: Internalized beliefs of inferiority, fear of failure, or low self-esteem can impede individuals' confidence and motivation to pursue empowerment, making it difficult for them to assert themselves and assert their rights.
- Lack of resources and opportunities: Scarcity of resources, such as financial capital, social networks, or access to healthcare and social services, can hinder individuals' ability to pursue their goals and fulfill their potential, perpetuating cycles of disempowerment and inequality

SUGGESTED GAME: EGG DROP

Needs: Raw eggs, masking tape, and drinking straws

Divide your group into teams and provide each team with a raw egg, a roll of masking tape, and drinking straws. Take the teams to a location where eggs can be dropped safely at least twenty feet. Inform the teams that they have 30 minutes to develop a way to drop the eggs without the egg breaking and start the clock. The team that completes the task using only the provided materials first wins. This competition requires communication, creativity, and open decision-making for success.

NOTES:

TEAM BUILDING
CHAPTER 16

DEFINITION

TEAM BUILDING MEANS working together to make your group stronger. Team building is important because it helps everyone in the group feel like they belong and can contribute their ideas and skills.

BIBLICAL REFERENCES

The Bible contains several passages that emphasize the importance of teamwork, collaboration, and unity among believers. Here are a few examples:

Ecclesiastes 4:9-12 (NIV):

> *"Two are better than one because they have a good return for their labor: If either of them falls down, one can help the other up. But pity anyone who falls and has no one to help them up. Also, if two lie down together, they will keep warm. But how can one keep warm alone? Though one may be overpowered, two can defend themselves. A cord of three strands is not quickly broken."*

Proverbs 27:17 (NIV):

> *"As iron sharpens iron, so one person sharpens another."*

Romans 12:4-5 (NIV):

> *"For just as each of us has one body with many members, and these members do not all have the same function, so in Christ we, though many, form one body, and each member belongs to all the others."*

1 Corinthians 12:12-27 (NIV): This passage uses the metaphor of the human body to illustrate the interconnectedness and interdependence of believers within the church, emphasiz-

ing the importance of each member working together for the common good.

Ephesians 4:16 (NIV):

> *"From him the whole body, joined and held together by every supporting ligament, grows and builds itself up in love, as each part does its work."*

These passages highlight the idea that working together as a team, supporting and encouraging one another, is essential for achieving common goals and fulfilling God's purposes.

Creating great teams involves several key factors that can help them work together effectively and achieve their goals. Here are some tips:

- Clear Goals: Make sure everyone on the team understands what the team is trying to accomplish. Having clear goals helps everyone stay focused and motivated.
- Communication: Encourage open and honest communication among team members. Listen to each other's ideas and opinions, and make sure everyone feels comfortable speaking up.
- Collaboration: Work together as a team to solve problems and complete tasks. Recognize and appreciate each team member's strengths and contributions.
- Respect: Treat each other with respect and kindness. Value each person's unique qualities and perspectives.
- Support: Be supportive of your teammates and offer help when needed. Show empathy and understanding towards others.
- Accountability: Hold yourself and your teammates accountable for your actions and commitments. Take responsibility for your role in the team's success.
- Celebrate Successes: Acknowledge and celebrate achievements, both big and small. Recognize the hard work and effort that everyone puts in.
- Learn from Mistakes: View mistakes as opportunities for learning and improvement. Encourage a growth mindset and embrace challenges as a team.
- Have Fun: Remember to enjoy the process of working together as a team. Foster a positive and enjoyable team environment.

By following these tips, you can help create a great team where everyone feels valued, supported, and motivated to do their best.

Discussion Questions: (Please limit to 4-5 questions that pertain to your group)

- Why is it important for team members to respect each other?
- How do you think having fun together as a team can improve overall teamwork and productivity?
- What are some ways to incorporate fun into team activities?
- Why do you think it's important for everyone in a group to feel like they belong and can share their ideas and skills?
- Can you tell about a time when you felt like you were part of a team?

- What are some important things for making a good team, according to the passage? Which one do you think is the most important, and why?
- How does having clear goals help a team to work together well?
- Can you think of a time when knowing what the group was trying to do helped everyone work better?
- Why is it important for people in a team to talk to each other?
- What does it mean to collaborate with others in a team?
- Can you give an example of a time when you worked with others to solve a problem or finish a project?
- Why is it important for team members to show respect to each other?
- Why is it good for team members to support each other?
- Why is it important for people in a team to be responsible for what they do?
- Can you tell about a time when everyone had to do their part for the group to succeed?

Information for Instructors

Barriers to team building are things that can get in the way of a group of people working well together. Here are some examples:

- Lack of Communication: When team members don't talk to each other or share their thoughts and ideas, it can be hard for everyone to understand what's going on and work together effectively.
- Conflict: If there are disagreements or arguments within the team, it can create tension and make it difficult for people to cooperate and collaborate.
- Trust Issues: When team members don't trust each other, they may hesitate to rely on one another or share important information, which can weaken the team's unity and effectiveness.
- Different Goals or Motivations: If team members have conflicting goals or motivations, they may not be aligned in their efforts, leading to confusion and frustration.
- Lack of Leadership: Without strong leadership or clear direction, team members may feel lost or unsure about what they're supposed to be doing, hindering their ability to work together cohesively.
- Cultural or Personality Differences: When team members come from different backgrounds or have different personalities, it can sometimes lead to misunderstandings or clashes that impede teamwork.

These barriers can make it challenging for teams to achieve their goals and function smoothly, but with awareness and effort, they can often be overcome through communication, conflict resolution, building trust, and fostering a shared sense of purpose.

SUGGESTED GAME: SILENT LINEUP

The group leader calls out, "Everyone, please now line up ..." and fills in the blank with a statement such as the suggestions below. All the players race to find the right order **without speaking.**

Ideas:

- Everyone please now line up in order of age, oldest at the front, youngest at the back
- Everyone please now line up in first name alphabet order
- Everyone please now line up by height, shortest first
- Everyone please now line up according to your birthday month and remember, no speaking
- Think of how many cousins have. Line up with the least cousins in front without speaking.
- Line up in alphabetical order of your middle name without speaking.

*feel free to play the game as many times as you want and add variations to the game.

NOTES:

MEDIATION
CHAPTER 17

DEFINITION

MEDIATION IS LIKE being a peacekeeper. When there's a problem or a fight between people, a mediator steps in to help them talk it out and find a solution. They listen to both sides and try to help them understand each other better. The goal is to find a fair and peaceful way to end the conflict so everyone feels satisfied.

BIBLICAL REFERENCES

In the Bible, mediation or mediating isn't explicitly mentioned in the modern sense of conflict resolution or negotiation. However, some passages reflect principles related to mediation, peace-keeping, and reconciliation:

Matthew 5:9 (New Testament):

‖   *"Blessed are the peacemakers, for they will be called children of God."*

This verse emphasizes the importance of promoting peace and resolving conflicts, which aligns with the goals of mediation.

Proverbs 15:18 (Old Testament):

‖   *"A hot-tempered person stirs up conflict, but the one who is patient calms a quarrel."*

This verse underscores the value of patience and peace in dealing with disputes, suggesting a form of mediation.

Matthew 18:15-17 (New Testament): This passage provides a process for addressing conflict within a community of believers, encouraging individuals to first address issues directly with one another and then involve additional parties if necessary, ultimately aiming for resolution and reconciliation.

1 Corinthians 6:1-8 (New Testament): In this passage, Paul admonishes believers for taking

their disputes before secular courts and encourages them to settle matters among themselves, implying a form of mediation or arbitration within the Christian community.

|| *While the term "mediation"*

may not be explicitly used in these passages, the principles of peacekeeping, reconciliation, and resolving conflicts through peaceful means are consistent with the concepts underlying mediation.

It can sometimes be tough to resolve conflicts through mediation, but with patience, understanding, and sometimes help from a mediator, it's possible to overcome them and find a peaceful resolution. By following the tips and practicing empathy and understanding, you can become better at mediation and help others resolve conflicts peacefully.

Discussion Questions: (Please limit to 4-5 questions that pertain to your group)

- Why is mediation important in resolving conflicts?
- Can you think of any tips that might be helpful in mediation?
- Imagine you're faced with a conflict between two friends. How might you apply the principles of mediation and the tips provided to help them find a solution and restore peace in their relationship?
- What qualities do you think make someone a good mediator?
- What does it mean to be a mediator, or a peacekeeper, when there's a problem?
- How does listening to both sides help in finding a solution?
- Why is it important for everyone in a problem to feel happy with the solution?
- How do the ideas of helping people talk out problems and finding peaceful ways to end fights relate to what the Bible teaches about making peace?
- Can you remember a time when you helped solve a problem between friends? What did you do, and how did it work out?
- Why do you think it's good to be someone who tries to make peace, according to what the Bible says in Matthew 5:9?
- How can being patient and trying to make peace, like it says in Proverbs 15:18, help us handle fights?
- How can we use the ideas of making peace and helping others talk out problems in our own lives and with our friends and family?

Tips for being a beetter mediator:

- Listen Carefully: Pay close attention to what each person involved in the conflict has to say. Listen without interrupting and try to understand their feelings and points of view.
- Stay Neutral: Be fair and impartial. Don't take sides or judge anyone. Your job is to help everyone involved find a solution that works for everyone.
- Be Patient: Conflict resolution takes time. Stay calm and patient, even if things get heated. Remember, it's normal for emotions to run high during mediation.
- Ask Questions: Encourage everyone to share their thoughts and feelings. Ask open-ended questions to help them explain their perspective and uncover the root of the problem.

- Find Common Ground: Look for areas where everyone can agree or compromise. Focus on shared interests and goals to find a solution that benefits everyone.
- Brainstorm Solutions: Encourage creative thinking. Help everyone involved come up with different ideas for resolving the conflict. Then, work together to find the best solution.
- Be Respectful: Treat everyone with kindness and respect, even if you disagree with them. Avoid blaming or criticizing anyone involved in the conflict.
- Follow Through: Once a solution is reached, make sure everyone understands their role and agrees to follow through with any commitments made during the mediation process.

INFORMATION FOR INSTRUCTORS

Barriers to mediation are things that can make it difficult for people to resolve conflicts peacefully. Here are some common Challenges:

- Lack of Communication: When people don't talk to each other or don't listen well, it's hard to understand each other's feelings and needs.
- Strong Emotions: Big feelings like anger or hurt can get in the way of finding a solution because they might make it hard to think clearly.
- Misunderstandings: Sometimes, people don't understand each other's perspectives or the reasons behind their actions, which can make it tough to find common ground.
- Power Imbalance: If one person has more control or influence than the other, it can be challenging to reach a fair agreement.
- Fear or Distrust: If people are afraid or don't trust each other, they may not be willing to work together to find a solution.
- Cultural or Language Differences: Different backgrounds or languages can make it harder for people to communicate effectively and understand each other's viewpoints.

SUGGESTED GAME: ROLE PLAY

*WARNING: Role play concerning conflict can still bring about REAL negative feelings among participants. My suggestion would be to allow the group to choose a game they enjoy and to use the meditation techniques during time away from the group, such as with friends who may need additional help during an argument.

Notes:

ACTIVE LISTENING
CHAPTER 18

DEFINITION

ACTIVE LISTENING MEANS really focusing on what someone is saying, not just hearing the words. It's like giving them your full attention, watching their face and body language, and trying to understand their feelings. Instead of just waiting for your turn to talk, you listen carefully and ask questions to show that you understand. It's a way to make sure both people really understand each other and feel heard.

BIBLICAL REFERENCES

In the Bible, several verses emphasize the importance of listening actively and attentively to others. Here are a few examples:

James 1:19 (NIV):

> *"My dear brothers and sisters, take note of this: Everyone should be quick to listen, slow to speak and slow to become angry."*

Proverbs 18:13 (NIV):

> *"To answer before listening— that is folly and shame."*

Proverbs 19:20 (NIV):

> *"Listen to advice and accept discipline, and at the end you will be counted among the wise."*

Matthew 13:9 (NIV):

> *"Whoever has ears, let them hear."*

Proverbs 1:5 (NIV):

> *"Let the wise listen and add to their learning, and let the discerning get guidance—"*

These verses emphasize the importance of being attentive listeners, being open to receiving advice and wisdom, and demonstrating patience in communication.

Building active listening skills is like learning any other skill — it takes practice and patience.

Here are some simple steps to help you improve your active listening skills:

1. Pay Attention: Focus on the person speaking, and try to ignore distractions like your phone or other thoughts.
2. Show You're Listening: Use body language to show you're paying attention. Face the speaker, nod occasionally, and make eye contact.
3. Don't Interrupt: Let the speaker finish what they're saying before you respond. Interrupting can make them feel like you're not really listening.
4. Paraphrase: After the speaker finishes, repeat what they said in your own words. This shows that you understand and helps clarify any misunderstandings.
5. Ask Questions: If you're not sure about something, ask questions to get more information or clarify what they meant.
6. Reflect Feelings: Try to understand how the speaker is feeling, and acknowledge their emotions. Saying things like "It sounds like you're really frustrated" shows empathy and encourages them to keep talking.
7. Give Feedback: Provide feedback to show that you're engaged in the conversation. You can say things like "I see what you mean" or "That makes sense."
8. Practice Active Silence: Sometimes, it's important to be silent and just listen. This gives the speaker space to think and express themselves fully.
9. Be Patient: Active listening takes time and effort. Be patient with yourself as you practice and improve your skills.

By practicing active listening, we can become better listeners and improve our communication with others. By following these steps and practicing active listening regularly, you can become better listeners and strengthen your relationships with others.

Discussion Questions: (Please limit to 4-5 questions that pertain to your group)

• How do you think active listening can help improve relationships between people?
• Can you identify any barriers in your own experiences communicating with others?
• Reflecting on the tips provided for building active listening skills, which one do you think you could work on the most?
• How can you show that you are actively listening to someone?
• Why is it important to pay attention to someone's body language when they are speaking?
• What does the Bible say about being quick to listen and slow to speak? (Hint: James 1:19)
• Why is it not wise to answer before listening, according to Proverbs 18:13?
• What does Proverbs 19:20 advise about listening to advice and discipline?

- Why do you think Jesus said, "Whoever has ears, let them hear" (Matthew 13:9)?
- How can repeating what someone said in your own words help in active listening?
- Why is it helpful to ask questions when you're listening to someone?
- How can acknowledging someone's feelings during a conversation show that you're actively listening?

INFORMATION FOR INSTRUCTORS

Challenges:

Barriers to active listening are like obstacles that can get in the way of really understanding what someone is saying. Here are a few common Challenges:

- Distractions: When your mind is focused on something else, like your phone or daydreaming, it's hard to pay attention to the person talking.
- Prejudice: If you already have a negative opinion about the speaker or their topic, you might not listen properly because you've already made up your mind.
- Assumptions: Sometimes, we think we know what someone is going to say before they finish talking. This can make us stop paying attention or jump to conclusions.
- Lack of Empathy: If you can't put yourself in the other person's shoes or understand how they're feeling, it's tough to really hear what they're saying.
- External Noise: When there's a lot of background noise or interruptions, it can be hard to focus on what's being said.
- Insecurity: If you're worried about how you'll respond or what you'll say next, you might not listen as well because you're too focused on yourself.

SUGGESTED GAME: SIMON SAYS

The players must obey all commands that begin with the words "Simon says." If Simon says, "Simon says touch your nose," then all players must touch their nose. However, if Simon says "jump" without saying "Simon says" first, the players must not jump. If they do jump, that player is out until the next game.

NOTES:

HUMILITY
CHAPTER 19

DEFINITION

HUMILITY MEANS BEING modest and not thinking you are better or more important than others. It's about being willing to listen and learn from others, admitting when you make mistakes, and not boasting or bragging about yourself. Humble people are respectful and kind to everyone; they understand that everyone has value and deserves respect.

BIBLICAL REFERENCES

Philippians 2:3-4 (NIV):

> *"Do nothing out of selfish ambition or vain conceit. Rather, in humility, value others above yourselves, not looking to your own interests but each of you to the interests of the others."*

James 4:6 (NIV):

> *"But he gives us more grace. That is why Scripture says: 'God opposes the proud but shows favor to the humble.'"*

1 Peter 5:5-6 (NIV):

> *"In the same way, you who are younger, submit yourselves to your elders. All of you, clothe yourselves with humility toward one another. because. 'God opposes the proud but shows favor to the humble.' Humble yourselves, therefore, under God's mighty hand, that he may lift you up in due time."*

Proverbs 22:4 (NIV):

> *"Humility is the fear of the Lord; its wages are riches and honor and life."*

These verses emphasize the importance of humility in the Christian faith, teaching that humility is valued by God and leads to blessings and favor from Him.

Building humility involves developing a mindset and behaviors that focus on valuing others, being open to learning, and recognizing your strengths and weaknesses without needing to prove yourself. Here are some simple ways to build humility:

- Listen actively: Pay attention when others are speaking and try to understand their perspectives without interrupting. This shows respect for their opinions and experiences.
- Admit mistakes: Be willing to acknowledge when you've made a mistake or when you don't know something. This shows humility and a willingness to learn and grow.
- Practice gratitude: Regularly take time to appreciate the people and things in your life. This helps you recognize that you're not alone and that others contribute to your success and happiness.
- Seek feedback: Ask for feedback from others about your actions and behavior. This shows that you value their input and are open to improving yourself.
- Serve others: Look for opportunities to help and support others without expecting anything in return. This demonstrates humility and a willingness to put others' needs before yours.
- Be open-minded: Stay open to new ideas and perspectives, even if they challenge your beliefs or opinions. This shows that you're willing to learn from others and consider different points of view.
- Practice empathy: Try to understand how others feel and show compassion towards their experiences. This helps you develop a deeper understanding of others and fosters humility.

Overcoming the barriers to humility involves being honest with yourself, valuing others, and being open to learning and growth. By incorporating the tips into your daily life, you can cultivate humility and develop a greater appreciation for others and their contributions.

Discussion Questions: (Please limit to 4-5 questions that pertain to your group)

- Why do you think humility is important in personal interactions and relationships?
- Can you think of any historical or contemporary leaders who exemplify humility?
- Think of a leader and ask yourself, how did their humility influence their leadership style and effectiveness?
- Why do you think humility is important in the Christian faith?
- Which of the tips for building humility do you think would be easiest for you to try? Why?
- Do you think it's possible for everyone to be humble? Why or why not?
- Why is it important to admit when we make mistakes? How does this relate to humility?
- What could be some barriers to humility, and how can we overcome them?
- Can you think of a character from a book or movie who shows humility? What qualities make them humble?
- Why do you think humility is often seen as a positive trait in people? What are the benefits of being humble?

Information for Instructors

Barriers to humility are things that can get in the way of being humble. Here are some common barriers to humility:

- Pride: Pride is when you think too highly of yourself and believe you are better than others. It can make it hard to admit when you're wrong or to see the value in others.
- Insecurity: Feeling insecure about yourself can make you want to prove yourself to others and seek validation. This can lead to boastful behavior and an unwillingness to admit mistakes.
- Fear of failure: If you're afraid of failing or being seen as weak, you might try to appear confident and perfect all the time. This can make it difficult to acknowledge your limitations and ask for help when you need it.
- Comparison: Comparing yourself to others can make you feel either superior or inferior. If you constantly compare yourself to those you perceive as less successful, you might become prideful. On the other hand, if you compare yourself to those you perceive as more successful, you might feel inadequate.
- Lack of empathy: Not understanding or caring about how others feel can prevent you from being humble. Empathy involves putting yourself in someone else's shoes and recognizing their experiences and feelings as valid.

Suggested Game: Pass it on!

You'll need an object that can be handed from one person to another easily, a timer, and a copy of this visible only to the organizer of the game: Z Y X W V U T S R Q P O N M L K J I H G F E D C B A.

Separate your group into teams and have them form single file lines. Hand the object to the first person in line and explain that you must say "A" and hand the object to the next person, where they will say "B" and pass it to the next player until you reach "Z" without dropping the object or missing a letter. If you drop the object or miss a letter, the object goes back to the first of the line, and you'll start again with the timer still going. You'll be timed, so you have to do it as quickly as possible. The team with the best time wins.

The first round should go smoothly… but then challenge both teams by saying, "Now, we're going to do it backward and start at Z." The game gets much more challenging and fun.

NOTES:

OPTIMISM
CHAPTER 20

DEFINITION

OPTIMISM IS LIKE wearing a pair of glasses that helps you see the bright side of things, even when stuff seems tough. It's about believing that good things can happen, even when there are challenges or problems. Optimistic people tend to focus on what they can control and look for solutions rather than dwelling on what's wrong. They believe in themselves and others, and they're hopeful about the future. Being optimistic doesn't mean ignoring problems, but it means facing them with a positive attitude and believing that things will get better.

BIBLICAL REFERENCES

In the Bible, there are several passages that can be interpreted as encouraging optimism or a positive outlook. Here are a few examples:

Philippians 4:13 (NIV):

> *"I can do all this through him who gives me strength."*

This verse suggests that with God's help, believers can overcome challenges and accomplish great things, instilling a sense of optimism and confidence.

Romans 8:28 (NIV):

> *"And we know that in all things God works for the good of those who love him, who have been called according to his purpose."*

This verse reminds believers that even in difficult circumstances, God works for their ultimate good, fostering hope and optimism.

Jeremiah 29:11 (NIV):

> *"For I know the plans I have for you,"*
> *declares the Lord, "plans to prosper you and not to harm you, plans to give you*
> *hope and a future."*

This verse emphasizes God's positive intentions for His people, offering them hope for the future and encouraging optimism.

Psalm 30:5 (NIV):

> *"For his anger lasts only a moment, but his favor lasts a lifetime; weeping may stay*
> *for the night, but rejoicing comes in the morning."*

This verse conveys the idea that even in times of sadness or difficulty, joy and comfort will eventually come, promoting optimism and trust in God's faithfulness.

These verses, among others in the Bible, highlight themes of hope, perseverance, and trust in God's promises, which can inspire optimism in the hearts of believers.

Tips on how to stay positive:

- Focus on the Good: instead of dwelling on what's wrong, try to look for the positives in every situation. Even when things seem tough, there's usually something good to be found if you look for it.
- Stay Positive: Try to maintain a positive attitude, even when faced with challenges. Believe that things will work out okay in the end, and try to see setbacks as temporary bumps on the road to success.
- Set Goals: Having goals gives you something to look forward to and work toward. Break big goals into smaller steps, and celebrate your progress along the way. This helps keep you motivated and optimistic about achieving your dreams.
- Practice Gratitude: Take time each day to think about what you're grateful for. This could be anything from a sunny day to spending time with loved ones. Practicing gratitude helps shift your focus to the good things in your life.
- Surround Yourself with Positive People: Spend time with friends and family who uplift and encourage you. Positive relationships can boost your mood and outlook on life, making it easier to stay optimistic.
- Learn from Challenges: Instead of seeing obstacles as roadblocks, think of them as opportunities to learn and grow. Every challenge you overcome makes you stronger and more resilient, which can increase your optimism for the future.
- Take Care of Yourself: Make sure to get enough sleep, eat healthily, and exercise regularly. Taking care of your physical and mental health can improve your overall outlook on life and help you stay optimistic.

Remember, being optimistic doesn't mean ignoring problems or pretending everything is perfect. It's about choosing to focus on the good, believing in yourself, and having hope for the future, even when things are tough.

Discussion Questions: (Please limit to 4-5 questions that pertain to your group)

- Will you share a time when you or someone you know demonstrated optimism during a tough time?
- How do you think optimism can impact our overall well-being and ability to cope with challenges?
- What steps can you take to enhance your own optimism moving forward?
- How do the Bible verses mentioned in the text encourage people to stay positive?
- Which tips for staying positive do you find most helpful or relatable?
- Can you think of any examples from your own life where these tips might have made a difference?
- Do you think it's easy or hard to be optimistic? Why or why not?
- Can you share any strategies you use to try to stay positive when things are tough?
- How do you think being around positive people can impact your own mood and outlook?
- Do you have friends or family members who make you feel more hopeful when you're with them?
- How do you think being healthy can help you feel more optimistic?
- Can you think of a time when you faced a problem but stayed positive about finding a solution?
- How do you think saying positive things to yourself can help you feel more optimistic?
- Why do you think being grateful for things in your life can help you stay positive?
- Can you name a few things you're grateful for right now?

INFORMATION FOR INSTRUCTORS

Challenges:

- Negative Thinking: Sometimes, we get stuck in a cycle of negative thoughts. We focus on what could go wrong instead of what could go right. This can make it hard to see the good in situations.
- Past Failures: When we've had bad experiences or failures in the past, it can be tough to believe that things will get better. We might think that because something went wrong before, it will always go wrong in the future.
- Fear of the Unknown: The future can seem scary because it's uncertain. We might worry about what could happen and imagine the worst-case scenarios, which makes it difficult to feel hopeful or optimistic.
- Surroundings and Influences: Sometimes, the people we're around or the things we see and hear can affect our outlook. If we're constantly surrounded by negativity or pessimism, it can be hard to stay positive.
- Self-Doubt: When we don't believe in ourselves or our abilities, it's challenging to feel optimistic about what we can achieve. Doubting ourselves can hold us back from seeing the potential for success.

- External Challenges: Outside factors like difficult circumstances or obstacles can make it tough to stay optimistic. When things are hard, it's natural to feel discouraged and find it hard to see a way forward.

Recognizing these barriers is the first step toward overcoming them. By challenging negative thoughts, learning from past experiences, focusing on possibilities, surrounding ourselves with positivity, building self-confidence, and finding support during tough times, we can work to cultivate a more optimistic outlook on life.

SUGGESTED GAME: DEBATE

Divide your group into two teams. One team will challenge the other team to respond to negative sentences. Each negative sentence must begin with the word I or MY. We don't want people hurling insults towards one another. The opposite team will respond by giving a positive reply to the negative statement. Statements can not be repeated by either team. The negative team will be allowed ten negative statements that are contradicted by the positive team. This game is quite fun if done correctly. The negative team will now become the positive team and vice/versa. They learn that there is always a positive in every situation.

NOTES:

HONESTY
CHAPTER 21

DEFINITION

HONESTY MEANS TELLING the truth and being sincere in what you say and do. It's about being genuine and trustworthy, not lying or cheating. Being honest means you're fair and reliable, and you own up to your mistakes instead of trying to hide them. It's important to be honest in your relationships with others and with yourself so people can trust and respect you.

BIBLICAL REFERENCES

The Bible contains several references to honesty and integrity. Here are a few examples:

Proverbs 12:22 (NIV):

> *"The Lord detests lying lips, but he delights in people who are trustworthy."*

Ephesians 4:25 (NIV):

> *"Therefore each of you must put off falsehood and speak truthfully to your neighbor, for we are all members of one body."*

Colossians 3:9-10 (NIV):

> *"Do not lie to each other, since you have taken off your old self with its practices and have put on the new self, which is being renewed in knowledge in the image of its Creator."*

Psalm 15:1-2 (NIV):

> *"Lord, who may dwell in your sacred tent? Who may live on your holy mountain? The one whose walk is blameless, who does what is righteous, who speaks the truth from their heart."*

These verses emphasize the importance of honesty and truthfulness in the eyes of God and in our relationships with others. They encourage believers to speak truthfully, avoid deceit, and live with integrity.

Being honest can be tough sometimes, but here are some simple steps to help:

1. Take a Deep Breath: When you're facing a difficult situation where honesty is important, take a moment to breathe and calm yourself down. It's okay to feel nervous or scared.
2. Think Before You Speak: Before you say anything, take a moment to think about what you want to say and why honesty is important in this situation. Consider the consequences of being dishonest.
3. Be Clear and Direct: When you're ready to speak, be clear and direct with your words. Say what you mean in a straightforward way without trying to sugarcoat or hide the truth.
4. Use "I" Statements: Instead of blaming others or making excuses, use "I" statements to take responsibility for your words and actions. For example, say, "I made a mistake" instead of "It's not my fault."
5. Stay Calm and Respectful: Even if the truth is difficult to hear, try to stay calm and respectful when you're talking to others. Avoid getting defensive or lashing out, and listen to what they have to say.
6. Apologize if Necessary: If your honesty involves admitting to something you did wrong, be prepared to apologize sincerely. Take responsibility for your actions and show that you're willing to make things right.
7. Practice Honesty Regularly: Honesty is like a muscle – the more you use it, the stronger it gets. Practice being honest in your everyday life, even when it's not easy, and it will become easier over time.

Remember, being honest might be hard at the moment, but it's worth it in the long run. It builds trust and respect in your relationships and helps you feel good about yourself.

Discussion Questions: (Please limit to 4-5 questions that pertain to your group)

- Can you think of a time when someone was honest with you, and how did it make you feel?
- Do you think being honest is important in everyday life?
- Why do you think it's sometimes hard to tell the truth?
- Can you share a situation where you found it difficult to be honest?
- Which step to being honest do you think would be the most helpful for you?
- Can you think of a time when someone's honesty strengthened your friendship with them?
- Why is it important to take responsibility for your actions, even when it's hard?
- How might being dishonest affect your friendships or how you feel about yourself?
- Can you think of ways you can practice being honest in your daily life?
- Do you think being honest gets easier the more you do it, like a muscle getting stronger? Why or why not?
- Can you think of any other skills that improve with practice?

- Have you ever been in a situation where someone wasn't honest with you? How did it make you feel, and what did you do about it?
- Why do you think honesty is seen as an important value in many cultures and religions?
- What do you think being honest says about a person's character?

Information for Instructors

Barriers to honesty:

- Fear of Consequences: Sometimes, people are afraid of getting into trouble or facing punishment if they tell the truth. They worry about what might happen to them if they admit to something wrong they've done.
- Peer Pressure: People might feel pressured to go along with what their friends or peers are saying or doing, even if it's not truthful. They might be afraid of being judged or left out if they don't go along with the group.
- Protecting Self-image: People often want to look good in front of others, so they might lie or exaggerate to make themselves seem better or more impressive than they really are. They worry that if they're honest about their flaws or mistakes, others won't like or respect them.
- Lack of Trust: If someone doesn't trust the person they're talking to, they might not feel comfortable being honest. They might worry that the other person will use the information against them or won't keep it confidential.
- Emotional Difficulty: Sometimes, telling the truth can be emotionally difficult, especially if it involves admitting to something painful or embarrassing. People might avoid being honest because they're afraid of facing those uncomfortable feelings.

These barriers can make it hard for people to be honest, even when they know it's the right thing to do.

Suggested Game: Two Truths and a Lie

On three pieces of paper, write a large letter A, B, and C on each of the papers. Place the papers on a table lying in the center of the room. The audience will be on one side of the table; the speaker will be on the opposite side. The first speaker will step behind the table, pick up the letter A, and make a statement. The speaker will move to the second and third papers, making a statement with each letter. One of the statements will be a lie. Only the participant will know which of the letters is the lie. The group will take turns guessing which statement is a lie.

You can keep score by noting which player confused the other participants the most times. The best liar wins, but it will assist all of the participants in measuring facial expressions and cognizing untruths.

NOTES:

Patience
Chapter 22

Definition

Patience is like waiting calmly without getting frustrated or upset. It's being able to stay calm and not rush when things take time or don't happen right away. Just like waiting for a plant to grow or for a friend to finish talking, patience means being able to wait without complaining or getting annoyed. It's an important skill that helps us deal with challenges and frustrations in a calm and positive way.

Biblical References

James 1:3-4 (NIV):

> *"Because you know that the testing of your faith produces perseverance. Let perseverance finish its work so that you may be mature and complete, not lacking anything."*

Romans 12:12 (NIV):

> *"Be joyful in hope, patient in affliction, faithful in prayer."*

Galatians 5:22-23 (NIV):

> *"But the fruit of the Spirit is love, joy, peace, forbearance, kindness, goodness, faithfulness, gentleness and self-control. Against such things, there is no law."*

Colossians 3:12 (NIV):

> *"Therefore, as God's chosen people, holy and dearly loved, clothe yourselves with compassion, kindness, humility, gentleness and patience."*

Hebrews 10:36 (NIV):

> *"You need to persevere so that when you have done the will of God, you will receive what he has promised."*

These verses emphasize the importance of patience as a virtue and its connection to faith, perseverance, and spiritual growth.

Tips:

- Take Deep Breaths: When you start feeling impatient, take a few deep breaths. It can help you calm down and think more clearly.
- Focus on the Present: Instead of worrying about what's going to happen next, try to focus on what's happening right now. It can help you stay grounded and patient.
- Practice Empathy: Try to understand other people's perspectives and why things might be taking longer than expected. It can help you be more patient with them.
- Find Distractions: If you're waiting for something, find something else to do to keep yourself busy. It can make the time go by faster and help you be more patient.
- Set Realistic Expectations: Understand that things don't always happen as quickly as we want them to. Setting realistic expectations can help you be more patient when things take longer than expected.
- Practice Gratitude: Focus on the good things in your life and things you're grateful for. It can help you stay positive and patient, even when things aren't going your way.
- Take Breaks: If you're feeling really impatient, take a break and come back to the situation later. Sometimes, a little time away can help you feel more patient and relaxed.

Remember, being patient is a skill that takes practice. Be kind to yourself and keep working on it, and you'll get better over time.

Discussion Questions: (Please limit to 4-5 questions that pertain to your group)

- Can you think of a time when you had to be patient? How did you handle it?
- Name a situation where you could apply one of these tips to be more patient?
- Why is it important to be patient with ourselves when learning new things or facing challenges?
- If you didn't have a phone with you for a distraction, what would be a way you could distract yourself while being patient?
- Do you think patience is important in our everyday lives?
- Can you share a situation where you found it difficult to wait calmly?
- What are some tips mentioned in the text to help you practice patience?
- Can you think of a time when understanding someone else's perspective helped you be more patient with them?
- Can you think of a time when practicing gratitude helped you stay patient in a difficult situation?
- Do you agree that being patient is a skill that takes practice? Why or why not?

- Can you think of any other skills that require practice to improve?
- Reflecting on the text and your own experiences, why do you think patience is considered a virtue?
- How might practicing patience contribute to personal growth and well-being?

Information for Instructors

Challenges:

There are several barriers that can make it difficult to be patient:

- Not Wanting to Wait: Sometimes, we just don't like waiting. We want things to happen right away.
- Feeling Stressed or Worried: When we're really stressed or worried, it's tough to stay calm and patient.
- Thinking Things Should Happen Faster: If we think things should happen quickly, we might get annoyed when they don't.
- Not Being in Control: It's hard to wait when we feel like we can't do anything to make things happen faster.
- Getting Distracted Easily: We can have trouble waiting if we're always distracted by other things going on.
- Worrying About Missing Out: Sometimes, we're scared of missing out on stuff, so we don't want to wait.
- Being Used to Getting Things Right Away: If we're used to getting what we want right away, it's harder to wait patiently.

Being patient means practicing waiting calmly, even when it's tough. It's something we can work on, but it takes practice and understanding.

Suggested Game: Hide and Go Seek

Use the traditional rules, no bases. All of the participants hide until found by the seeker. The last one that is found or not found wins the game. The participants who are waiting must wait patiently to be found.

NOTES:

Time Management
Chapter 23

Definition

TIME MANAGEMENT MEANS using your time wisely. It's about planning what you need to do and deciding what's most important. When you manage your time well, you can get things done without feeling rushed or stressed. It's like making a schedule for your day and sticking to it so you can finish your homework and chores and still have time for fun stuff.

Biblical References

In the Bible, there are several verses that can be interpreted as advocating for principles of time management.

Ecclesiastes 3:1-8: This passage famously speaks about there being a time for everything under the heavens - a time to be born and a time to die, a time to plant and a time to uproot, etc. It emphasizes the importance of recognizing and respecting the timing of events in life.

Psalm 90:12:

> *"Teach us to number our days, that we may gain a heart of wisdom."*

This verse encourages individuals to be mindful of the limited time they have on Earth and to use it wisely.

Colossians 4:5:

> *"Be wise in the way you act toward outsiders; make the most of every opportunity."*

This verse advises believers to make the most of their time and opportunities by acting wisely and thoughtfully.

Proverbs 13:4:

> *"The sluggard craves and gets nothing, but the desires of the diligent are fully satisfied."*

This proverb contrasts laziness with diligence, suggesting that managing time well leads to fulfillment and success.

Matthew 6:34:

> *"Therefore do not worry about tomorrow, for tomorrow will worry about itself. Each day has enough trouble of its own."*

This verse encourages living in the present moment and focusing on one day at a time, which is a principle often emphasized in time management techniques.

While these verses may not explicitly address modern concepts of time management, they contain wisdom and principles that can be applied to effectively manage one's time and priorities.

Tips on managing time better:

- Make a to-do list: Write down all the things you need to do and check them off as you finish each one. This helps you stay organized and focused.
- Prioritize tasks: Determine which tasks are most important or urgent, and do those first. This way, you'll tackle the important stuff before it becomes overwhelming.
- Break tasks into smaller steps: Big tasks can seem daunting, but breaking them down into smaller, manageable steps makes them easier to handle.
- Set deadlines: Give yourself deadlines for completing tasks, even if they're not required. This keeps you motivated and helps you stay on track.
- Use a planner or calendar: Write down important dates, deadlines, and appointments so you don't forget them. This helps you plan your time effectively and avoid last-minute rushes.
- Minimize distractions: Find a quiet, distraction-free space to work in, and turn off notifications on your phone or computer while you're working.
- Take breaks: It's important to take regular breaks to rest and recharge. This can help you stay focused and productive when you're working.
- Learn to say no: If you're already busy or overwhelmed, it's okay to say no to extra tasks or requests. Don't take on more than you can handle.
- Stay organized: Keep your workspace tidy and organized so you can find what you need quickly and easily. This saves time and reduces stress.
- Review and adjust: Periodically review your to-do list and schedule to see what's working and what's not. Adjust your approach as needed to improve your time management skills over time.

Discussion Questions: (Please limit to 4-5 questions that pertain to your group)

- Can you think of a time when managing your time well helped you accomplish something important?
- Can you explain how the verses listed above might offer guidance on using time wisely?
- Why do you think managing time well is important?
- Can you share an example of a time when poor time management led to stress or difficulty?

- Which tip for managing time better do you think would be the most helpful for you personally?
- How might making a to-do list help you stay organized and focused?
- Can you think of any other ways to keep track of tasks and priorities?
- Can you share a time when prioritizing tasks helped you accomplish more in a day?
- What are some common distractions that can interfere with time management?
- Can you think of any ways you could improve your current approach to managing time?
- Do you think effective time management is a valuable skill to develop?
- How might improving your time management skills benefit you in the future?

INFORMATION FOR INSTRUCTORS

Here are some common barriers to time management:

- Procrastination: This means putting off tasks until later instead of doing them now. It can make you feel stressed and overwhelmed when deadlines start looming.
- Distractions: These are things that take your attention away from what you're supposed to be doing, like your phone buzzing with notifications or friends chatting with you when you're trying to work.
- Poor planning: Not making a plan or setting goals for what you need to do can make it hard to know where to start or how to use your time wisely.
- Taking on too much: Trying to do too many things at once can make it hard to focus and get things done well.
- Not saying no: Sometimes, you need to turn down extra tasks or requests so you don't overload yourself with work.
- Being disorganized: If your things are all over the place or you don't have a system for keeping track of assignments and deadlines, it can be hard to manage your time effectively.
- Fear of failure: Being afraid that you won't do something perfectly can hold you back from starting or finishing tasks on time.
- Waiting for the perfect moment: If you're always waiting for things to be just right before you start working, you might never get started at all.
- Being too hard on yourself: Putting too much pressure on yourself to be perfect or to do everything perfectly can make it hard to manage your time in a healthy way.
- Not asking for help: Sometimes, it's okay to ask for help or advice when you're struggling with managing your time.

SUGGESTED GAME: HOW LONG IS A MINUTE?

While using a timer, instruct your group to shut their eyes and to open their eyes when they think 60 seconds have passed. Some people will open their eyes before the 60 seconds are up, and some will open them after. This quick game helps players better estimate the time it takes to finish projects and tasks because they'll understand how they perceive time.

Second Suggested Game: $86,400

Give each player a piece of paper and a writing tool. Each member of your team is instructed that they will be given $86,400 to spend within one day. Anything you don't spend is lost, and you can't carry over what you didn't spend today to tomorrow. Have everyone write down what activities they want to spend this money on.

Your team learns that the $86,400 you are given to spend is actually 86,400 seconds you have per day. The group learns that, instead of money, it's actually time that you won't be able to retrieve it tomorrow if you lose it today.

NOTES:

VISION
CHAPTER 24

DEFINITION

HAVING A VISION for your life means having a clear picture of what you want to achieve in the future. It's like having a big dream or goal that you're working towards. It helps you make decisions and take actions that will lead you in the direction you want to go. Having a vision can give you a sense of purpose and motivation to keep going, even when things get tough. It's like having a roadmap for where you want your life to go.

BIBLICAL REFERENCES

There are several biblical references to having a vision for your life:

Proverbs 29:18 (NIV):

> *"Where there is no revelation, people cast off restraint; but blessed is the one who heeds wisdom's instruction."*

This verse suggests that having a vision or revelation of God's wisdom leads to blessings and guidance in life.

Habakkuk 2:2-3 (NIV):

> *"Then the Lord replied: 'Write down the revelation and make it plain on tablets so that a herald may run with it. For the revelation awaits an appointed time; it speaks of the end and will not prove false. Though it linger, wait for it; it will certainly come and will not delay.'"*

Here, the importance of writing down and holding onto a vision, even if it takes time to come to fruition, is emphasized.

Proverbs 16:3 (NIV):

> *"Commit to the Lord whatever you do, and he will establish your plans."*

This verse encourages individuals to align their visions and plans with God's will, trusting in His guidance and direction.

Jeremiah 29:11 (NIV):

> *"'For I know the plans I have for you,' declares the Lord, 'plans to prosper you and not to harm you, plans to give you hope and a future.'"*

This well-known verse assures believers that God has a specific plan and vision for each person's life, one that brings hope and a promising future.

These verses illustrate the biblical concept of having a vision for one's life that is grounded in faith and aligned with God's purpose and guidance. Remember, creating a vision for your life is about imagining the kind of future you want and taking steps to make it a reality. It's okay to start small and make adjustments along the way. Just keep moving forward with determination and a positive attitude, and you'll be on your way to turning your vision into reality.

Steps to developing a vision for your life:

1. Imagine Your Future: Close your eyes and think about what you want your life to be like in the future. Picture yourself happy, successful, and fulfilled.
2. Discover Your Passions: What are the things that make you excited and happy? Whether it's art, sports, science, or helping others, identify your passions.
3. Set Goals: Think about what you want to achieve in different areas of your life, like school, career, relationships, and personal growth. Make specific goals that you can work towards.
4. Write it Down: Take a piece of paper and write down your vision for your life. Describe what you want to accomplish and how you want to feel.
5. Break it Down: Break your vision into smaller steps or goals. This makes it easier to achieve them one by one.
6. Stay Positive: Believe in yourself and your abilities. Don't let negative thoughts or doubts hold you back.
7. Take Action: Start taking small steps towards your goals. Whether it's studying harder, practicing a skill, or volunteering, every action counts.
8. Stay Flexible: Life may not always go as planned, and that's okay. Be open to new opportunities and willing to adjust your vision if needed.
9. Find Support: Surround yourself with people who encourage and support you. They can help you stay motivated and overcome challenges.
10. Keep Dreaming: Your vision for your life may change over time, and that's normal. Keep dreaming and setting new goals as you grow and learn more about yourself and the world around you.

Discussion Questions: (Please limit to 4-5 questions that pertain to your group)

- What does it mean to have a vision for your life?
- How can having a clear vision for your future help you make decisions in the present?

- Why is it important to align your vision with your authentic self rather than being influenced by others' expectations?
- Can you share a dream or goal you have for your future?
- Can you explain how the verses mentioned might inspire or guide someone in creating their own vision?
- Why do you think having a vision for your life is important?
- Can you think of any examples from your own life or the lives of others where having a clear vision helped someone achieve their goals?
- Which step to creating a vision for your life do you think would be the most challenging or most exciting for you to try?
- How might discovering your passions help you create a vision for your life?
- Can you share some of your own passions and how they might influence your future goals?
- Why is it important to stay positive when working towards your vision for your life?
- How might a positive attitude impact your ability to overcome obstacles and achieve your goals?
- Reflecting on the steps provided in the text, which one do you think is the most crucial for turning your vision into reality? Can you explain why you think this step is particularly important?
- How might your vision for your life change and evolve over time?
- Can you think of any ways you could adapt to these changes while still staying true to your core values and aspirations?

INFORMATION FOR INSTRUCTORS

Creating a vision for your life can be a deeply personal and introspective process, but it can also be challenging due to various barriers. Here are some common barriers you might encounter:

- Being Uncertain: Uncertainty about what you truly want can hinder the visioning process. If you're unsure about your values, passions, or long-term goals, it's difficult to create a clear vision for your life.
- Fear of Failure: The fear of making the wrong choices or failing to achieve your envisioned future can hold you back from dreaming big or committing to a particular vision.
- Influence from others: External Influences: Pressure from family, friends, society, or cultural expectations can steer you away from creating a vision that aligns with your authentic self. It's important to filter out external noise and focus on what truly matters to you.
- Lack of Confidence: Negative self-talk and limiting beliefs about your abilities, worthiness, or possibilities can sabotage your efforts to create a compelling vision for your life. Overcoming these beliefs is crucial for personal growth and transformation.
- Past Experiences: Traumatic or negative experiences from the past can cloud your vision and make it challenging to imagine a brighter future. It's essential to heal from past wounds and cultivate a mindset of resilience and optimism.
- Procrastination: Putting off the visioning process due to busyness, laziness, or a lack of

commitment can prevent you from taking proactive steps toward creating the life you desire. Overcoming procrastination requires discipline and a willingness to prioritize self-discovery and personal development.

- Feeling Overwhelmed: The sheer magnitude of envisioning your entire life can feel overwhelming, leading to avoidance or paralysis. Breaking down the process into smaller, manageable steps can help make it more approachable and achievable.
- Circumstances: Unforeseen events or circumstances beyond your control, such as financial setbacks, health issues, or relationship challenges, can disrupt your vision and force you to adapt or revise your plans.
- Perfectionism: Striving for perfection in your vision can be paralyzing and unrealistic. Embracing imperfection and allowing room for growth, flexibility, and experimentation can make the visioning process more enjoyable and sustainable.
- Lack of Support: Surrounding yourself with people who don't understand or support your vision can make it harder to stay motivated and committed. Seek out mentors, coaches, or like-minded individuals who can offer encouragement, guidance, and accountability.

Overcoming these barriers requires self-awareness, resilience, and a willingness to step out of your comfort zone. Remember that creating a vision for your life is an ongoing journey, and it's okay to adjust and refine your vision as you grow and evolve.

SUGGESTED GAME: BUILD A GOAL LADDER

Provide each person with a pencil and paper. The idea is to draw a ladder. On the top rung of the ladder, they will write an "ultimate goal." Each rung under the ladder will be a breakdown of goals that have to be accomplished in order to reach the top rung. Have them leave room between the rungs in order to add rungs if they think of another goal and have to add a rung.

Have them think about the barriers to their goals and develop ladder rungs that battle the barriers. Have fun discussing goals and barriers as a group.

The bottom of the ladder should be items such as eating right, staying safe, and getting enough sleep. Challenge your group to be as detailed as possible while focusing on the end goal. The idea behind the game is to challenge the student to think in stages to their ultimate goal.

Notes:

SELF-AWARENESS
CHAPTER 25

DEFINITION

SELF-AWARENESS MEANS UNDERSTANDING yourself - knowing your thoughts, feelings, and why you do things. It's like looking at yourself from the inside out, knowing what makes you happy, sad, or angry. When you're self-aware, you can see how your actions affect yourself and others, and you can make better choices because of it. It's like having a mirror for your thoughts and emotions, helping you understand who you are and how you fit into the world around you.

BIBLICAL REFERENCES

In the Bible, there are several references to the concept of self-awareness, often framed within the context of introspection, understanding one's actions, and recognizing one's relationship with God and others. Here are a few examples:

Proverbs 4:23 (NIV):

> *"Above all else, guard your heart, for everything you do flows from it."*

This verse emphasizes the importance of self-awareness, suggesting that one's actions stem from the condition of one's heart, encouraging individuals to be mindful of their inner thoughts and feelings.

Psalm 139:23-24 (NIV):

> *"Search me, God, and know my heart; test me and know my anxious thoughts. See if there is any offensive way in me, and lead me in the way everlasting."*

This passage reflects a prayer for self-awareness, asking God to reveal any hidden or harmful aspects within oneself and to guide the individual towards a righteous path.

James 1:23-25 (NIV):

> *"Anyone who listens to the word but does not do what it says is like someone who looks at his face in a mirror and, after looking at himself, goes away and immediately forgets what he looks like. But whoever looks intently into the perfect law that gives freedom and continues in it—not forgetting what they have heard, but doing it—they will be blessed in what they do."*

This passage uses the metaphor of a mirror to illustrate the importance of self-awareness in relation to one's actions and adherence to God's teachings.

1 Corinthians 11:28 (NIV):

> *"Everyone ought to examine themselves before they eat of the bread and drink from the cup."*

This verse highlights the practice of self-examination before partaking in communion, emphasizing the importance of introspection and awareness of one's spiritual state.

These verses underscore the significance of self-awareness in a spiritual context, urging individuals to reflect on their thoughts, intentions, and behaviors in relation to their faith and moral values.

Tips to being more self aware:

- Pay Attention to Feelings: Take some time each day to notice how you're feeling. Are you happy, sad, excited, or worried? Understanding your emotions can help you understand yourself better.

- Reflect on Your Actions: Think about the things you do and why you do them. Are your actions in line with your values and goals? If not, why? Reflecting on your choices can help you learn more about yourself.

- Ask for Feedback: Talk to trusted friends, family members, or teachers and ask them what they think about you. Their perspective can help you see yourself from a different angle.

- Keep a Journal: Writing down your thoughts and feelings can help you organize your thoughts and track patterns in your behavior. It's like having a conversation with yourself on paper.

- Practice Mindfulness: Take moments throughout the day to focus on the present moment. Pay attention to your senses - what you see, hear, smell, taste, and feel. This can help you stay grounded and aware of yourself.

- Set Goals: Think about what you want to achieve in different areas of your life, like school, sports, or hobbies. Setting goals can give you direction and help you understand what's important to you.

- Learn from Mistakes: Instead of beating yourself up over mistakes, try to see them as opportunities for growth. What can you learn from this experience? How can you do better next time?

Recognizing the barriers to self-awareness is the first step toward overcoming them and becoming more self-aware. It's like clearing away obstacles so we can see ourselves more clearly and understand who we truly are. Remember, building self-awareness is a journey, and it's okay to take it one step at a time. The more you practice the tips listed, the more you'll understand yourself and what makes you tick.

Discussion Questions: (Please limit to 4-5 questions that pertain to your group)

- Can you think of a time when you were aware of your own thoughts and feelings?
- How do the Bible verses mentioned in the text relate to understanding oneself?
- Can you explain how the verses listed encourage thinking about your actions and feelings?
- Why is understanding yourself important?
- Can you share an example of how knowing your own feelings helped you make a decision?
- Which tip for being more self-aware do you think would be the most helpful for you to try?
- How might paying attention to your feelings help you understand yourself better?
- Can you think of a time when understanding your emotions helped you handle a problem?
- Why is it important to think about the things you do and why you do them?
- Can you share a time when thinking about your actions helped you understand yourself better?
- How might talking to trusted friends or family members help you understand yourself?
- Can you think of a time when someone else's perspective helped you understand yourself better?
- Why do you think keeping a journal can be helpful for understanding yourself?
- Can you imagine how writing down your thoughts and feelings might help you learn more about yourself?
- Which tip to being more self aware do you think might be the hardest for you to try, why it's the hardest and how you might overcome it?
- How do you think understanding yourself better can help you in school and in your relationships with others?
- Can you think of ways being more self-aware might make your life better?

INFORMATION FOR INSTRUCTORS

Being self-aware can sometimes be tricky. Here are a few things that might get in the way of being self-aware:

- Not Paying Attention to Feelings: Sometimes, we're so busy with our day-to-day activities that we don't stop to think about how we're feeling. It's like being on autopilot and not noticing what's going on inside us.
- Ignoring Mistakes: When we make mistakes, it can be tempting to brush them off or blame someone else. But being self-aware means facing up to our mistakes and learning from them instead of pretending they didn't happen.
- Peer Pressure: Friends and classmates can have a big influence on us, and sometimes, we

might do things just to fit in, even if it's not really what we want. This can make it hard to know our true selves.

- Fear of Judgment: It's natural to worry about what others think of us, but this fear can stop us from being honest with ourselves. We might hide our true feelings or opinions because we're afraid of being judged.
- Lack of Reflection: Taking time to think about our thoughts, feelings, and actions is important for self-awareness. But with all the distractions around us, like social media and video games, it's easy to forget to pause and reflect.

SUGGESTED GAME: THE SHARE CIRCLE

With participants in a circle, ask them to complete the sentences listed. Participants can answer some or all of the questions. If you have a small group, you can ask each group member to answer the questions. If you have a larger group, go around the circle one at a time and ask individuals different questions.

I feel angry when…

I feel joyful when…

I feel unhappy when…

I feel hope when…

I wish I didn't have to…

I enjoy…

I feel afraid when…

Something I'd like to change is…

If I were (name a person), I would…

I feel like no one loves me when…

I know I am loved when…

Something I find boring is…

I know I can trust…

I admire (name a person) because…

I feel serene when…

I am most interested in….

I am annoyed when…

I disapprove of…

I am optimistic when

NOTES:

SELF-MOTIVATION
CHAPTER 26

DEFINITION

SELF-MOTIVATION IS WHEN you feel inspired or driven to do something without needing someone else to push you. It's like having your own engine inside you that keeps you going even when things get tough. You find reasons within yourself to work hard and keep trying, whether it's to achieve a goal, learn something new, or improve yourself. It's about believing in yourself and your abilities and finding the energy and determination to keep moving forward, even when obstacles come your way.

BIBLICAL REFERENCES

While the term "self-motivation" may not be explicitly mentioned in the Bible, there are principles and teachings that encourage individuals to take initiative, persevere, and remain steadfast in their faith and actions. Here are a few biblical references that align with the concept of self-motivation:

Proverbs 6:6-8 (NIV):

> *"Go to the ant, you sluggard; consider its ways and be wise! It has no commander, no overseer or ruler, yet it stores its provisions in summer and gathers its food at harvest."*

This passage highlights the importance of being proactive and diligent, using the example of the ant, which works without external supervision.

2 Timothy 1:7 (NIV):

> *"For the Spirit God gave us does not make us timid, but gives us power, love, and self-discipline."*

This verse suggests that God provides believers with the strength and self-discipline needed to pursue their goals and overcome challenges.

Philippians 2:12-13 (NIV):

> *"Therefore, my dear friends, as you have always obeyed—not only in my presence, but now much more in my absence—continue to work out your salvation with fear and trembling, for it is God who works in you to will and to act in order to fulfill his good purpose."*

Here, believers are encouraged to actively work out their faith, indicating a personal responsibility to grow and persevere in their spiritual journey.

Galatians 6:4-5 (NIV):

> *"Each one should test their own actions. Then they can take pride in themselves alone, without comparing themselves to someone else, for each one should carry their own load."*

This passage emphasizes individual accountability and encourages self-reflection and self-improvement without comparing oneself to others.

While these verses don't explicitly use the term "self-motivation," they promote the idea of taking personal responsibility, being diligent, relying on God's strength, and pursuing goals with determination—a mindset that aligns with the concept of self-motivation.

Here are some tips to become more self-motivated:

- Set Clear Goals: Start by setting specific, achievable goals for yourself. Think about what you want to accomplish and break it down into smaller steps. Having clear goals gives you something to work towards and helps you stay focused.
- Find Your Why: Understand why your goals are important to you. Knowing the reasons behind your goals can help you stay motivated, especially when things get tough. Think about how achieving your goals will benefit you in the long run.
- Create a Plan: Once you have your goals, make a plan for how you'll achieve them. Break down your goals into smaller tasks and set deadlines for each task. Having a plan in place makes it easier to stay organized and track your progress.
- Stay Positive: Replace negative thoughts with positive affirmations. When you catch yourself thinking things like "I can't do this," challenge those thoughts and replace them with more positive ones, like "I can do this if I put my mind to it." Positive thinking can help boost your confidence and motivation.
- Take Action: Don't wait for motivation to strike; sometimes, you have to take action first. Start working on your goals, even if you don't feel motivated at first. Once you get started, you'll often find that motivation follows.
- Reward Yourself: Celebrate your accomplishments along the way. When you reach a milestone or complete a task, reward yourself with something you enjoy, like a treat or a break. Rewarding yourself helps reinforce positive behaviors and keeps you motivated to keep going.
- Stay Persistent: Remember that success often requires perseverance. Don't let setbacks or

obstacles discourage you. Keep pushing forward, even when things get tough. Remember that every step you take brings you closer to your goals.

- Seek Support: Surround yourself with supportive people who believe in you and your goals. Share your goals with friends, family, or mentors who can offer encouragement and guidance. Having a support system can help keep you motivated, especially during challenging times.

By following the tips and staying committed to your goals, you can become more self-motivated and achieve success in whatever you set out to do.

Discussion Questions: (Please limit to 4-5 questions that pertain to your group)

- Can you think of a time when you felt really determined to do something on your own?
- How do the Bible verses mentioned relate to doing things without needing someone else to push you?
- Can you explain how these verses encourage people to be strong and keep trying, even when things are tough?
- Why do you think it's important to be able to motivate yourself?
- Can you share a time when you needed to keep going even when it was hard?
- Which tip for becoming more self-motivated do you think you could try to help you do things on your own?
- How might setting clear goals help you stay motivated?
- Why is it important to understand why your goals are important to you?
- Can you think of something you want to do and why it's important to you?
- How can staying positive help you stay motivated?
- Can you think of a time when staying positive helped you keep going even when things were tough?
- Why is taking action important for self-motivation?
- Can you think of something you did even when you didn't feel like it, but it helped you get started?
- How might rewarding yourself for accomplishing goals make you want to keep going?
- Can you think of a way you could reward yourself for finishing something you've been working on?
- Why do you think it's important to keep trying, even when things get tough?
- Can you share a time when you didn't give up and you felt really proud of yourself afterward?

INFORMATION FOR INSTRUCTORS

Barriers to being self-motivated:

- Fear of Failure: One big barrier to self-motivation is the fear of not succeeding. When we worry too much about failing, it can stop us from even trying. Overcoming this fear means learning to accept that mistakes are part of the learning process.

- Lack of Clear Goals: If we don't have a clear idea of what we want to achieve or how to get there, it's like trying to navigate without a map. Setting specific and achievable goals helps us stay focused and motivated.
- Negative Self-Talk: When we constantly criticize ourselves or doubt our abilities, it's like having a negative voice in our heads dragging us down. Learning to challenge these negative thoughts and replace them with positive affirmations can help boost our motivation.
- Procrastination: Putting off tasks or delaying action is a common barrier to self-motivation. We might procrastinate because we're afraid of failure or because the task feels overwhelming. Breaking tasks into smaller, manageable steps and setting deadlines can help overcome procrastination
- Lack of Support: Having someone to encourage and support us can make a big difference in staying motivated. Without that support, it's easy to feel like we're on our own and lose motivation.
- Feeling Overwhelmed: When we have too much to do and not enough time or resources, it can feel like we're drowning. Learning to prioritize tasks and break them down into smaller steps can make them feel more manageable.
- Lack of Passion: If we're not passionate about our goals or the tasks we need to accomplish, it's hard to stay motivated. Finding activities or projects that genuinely interest and excite us can help reignite our motivation.
- Physical or Mental Health Issues: Physical or mental health challenges, such as fatigue, anxiety, or depression, can drain our energy and make it difficult to stay motivated. Taking care of our health and seeking support when needed is crucial for maintaining motivation.

SUGGESTED GAME: HOW LONG CAN YOU GO ON

This game involves two or more persons. In this game, the participants balance the pen between their nostrils and upper lip. The participants have to wedge the pencil between this space in a 'smooch' position while they tilt their heads a little bit backward. The participant who can hold the pen or pencil the longest wins.

Spectators can throw sarcasm, jokes, and taunts to see who gets distracted first. You could ask the participating employees to pass through a series of barricades and things like that to see who will manage to keep the pencil in its place. The inability to hold the pen for a long time indicates a lack of focus in a stressful situation.

NOTES:

Positively Motivating Others
Chapter 27

Definition

Positively motivating others means encouraging them in a cheerful and supportive way to do their best and reach their goals. It's like being a friendly cheerleader, giving them a boost of energy and confidence to keep going and believe in themselves. When you positively motivate someone, you make them feel good about what they're doing and help them stay excited and focused on their tasks or dreams. So, it's all about spreading positivity and encouragement to inspire others to succeed.

Biblical References

The Bible contains several passages that emphasize the importance of encouraging and positively motivating others. Here are a few examples:

Hebrews 10:24-25 (NIV):

> *"And let us consider how we may spur one another on toward love and good deeds, not giving up meeting together, as some are in the habit of doing, but encouraging one another—and all the more as you see the Day approaching."*

1 Thessalonians 5:11 (NIV):

> *"Therefore encourage one another and build each other up, just as in fact you are doing."*

Proverbs 16:24 (NIV):

> *"Gracious words are a honeycomb, sweet to the soul and healing to the bones."*

Ephesians 4:29 (NIV):

> *"Do not let any unwholesome talk come out of your mouths, but only what is helpful for building others up according to their needs, that it may benefit those who listen."*

Colossians 3:16 (NIV):

> *"Let the message of Christ dwell among you richly as you teach and admonish one another with all wisdom through psalms, hymns, and songs from the Spirit, singing to God with gratitude in your hearts."*

These verses encourage believers to speak words of encouragement, build each other up, and motivate one another to love and do good deeds, reflecting biblical teachings.

Tips for positively motivating other people:

- Give Encouragement: Tell others they're doing a great job and that you believe in them. Encouraging words can boost their confidence and make them feel good about themselves.
- Be Supportive: Show that you're there for them by offering help and listening to their concerns. Knowing they have someone to turn to can make a big difference in their motivation.
- Set Goals Together: Work with them to set achievable goals. Break big tasks into smaller steps, and celebrate each accomplishment along the way. This helps them see progress and stay motivated.
- Lead by Example: Show enthusiasm and positivity in your own actions. When others see your excitement and determination, it can inspire them to do the same.
- Provide Constructive Feedback: Offer feedback in a kind and helpful way. Point out what they're doing well and offer suggestions for improvement. This shows that you care about their progress and want to see them succeed.
- Create a Positive Environment: Surround them with positivity and encouragement. Avoid negative comments or criticism and instead focus on uplifting them and building their confidence.
- Celebrate Successes: When they reach a goal or accomplish something they've been working towards, celebrate it! Whether it's a small achievement or a big milestone, celebrating success reinforces their motivation and encourages them to keep going.

Discussion Questions: (Please limit to 4-5 questions that pertain to your group)

- Can you give an example of receiving positive motivation from your own experience?
- How do you think encouraging words can impact a person's confidence and motivation?
- Why do you think it's important to be supportive of others, especially when they're facing challenges or feeling stressed?
- What are some barriers that can prevent people from feeling motivated?
- In the Bible verses we read, what do you think the message is about?
- How can we encourage each other in our daily lives, like the verses suggest?

- What's a good way to give feedback to help someone do better without making them feel bad?
- How can we make our classroom or group a positive and encouraging place for everyone?
- What are some things we can do to support each other?
- Why do you think it's important to be kind and supportive to others, even when we might be feeling upset or frustrated ourselves?
- How can we show that we appreciate and care for our friends and classmates?
- What are some ways we can lift each other up and spread positivity every day?

INFORMATION FOR INSTRUCTORS

Challenges:

- Negative Attitude: Sometimes, if someone has a bad attitude, it can be hard to motivate them because they might not want to listen or try new things.
- Lack of Interest: If a person isn't interested in what you're trying to motivate them to do, they might not feel motivated to do it.
- Feeling Overwhelmed: When someone has too much to do or feels like they can't handle everything, they might not be open to motivation because they're already stressed.
- Personal Problems: If someone is dealing with personal issues like family problems or feeling upset, it can be hard for them to focus on being motivated.
- Fear of Failure: Sometimes, people are scared to try something new because they're afraid they'll fail. This fear can stop them from feeling motivated to even give it a try.
- Lack of Confidence: If someone doesn't believe in themselves or their abilities, they might not feel motivated because they don't think they can succeed.

Understanding the barriers to positively motivating others can help us find ways to overcome them and find the right approach to motivate others. It's important to be patient, understanding, and supportive when trying to motivate others. By following these tips, you can help positively motivate others and support them in reaching their goals. Remember, a little encouragement can go a long way!

SUGGESTED GAME: CONCENTRATION

Participants will need to form two equal lines facing each other. One line turns around, giving the second line 30 seconds to change ten things about themselves. After 30 seconds, the first group turns around and tries to find all the changes the other group made.

NOTES:

GIVING AND RECEIVING FEEDBACK
CHAPTER 28

DEFINITION

FEEDBACK IS A helpful tip or comment about something you've done. It's a way to learn and improve. Feedback is a positive form of what some may call criticism, but feedback is a positive way of helping someone improve without offering negative comments.

Giving Feedback: When you give feedback, be kind and specific. Instead of saying, "Good job!" try saying what you liked and why. For example, "I really liked how you explained your ideas clearly. It made it easy to understand."

Receiving Feedback: When you get feedback, listen carefully and thank the person. Even if it's something you don't agree with, try to understand their point of view. Then, think about how you can use the feedback to do better next time. For example, if someone says your writing could be clearer, you can work on making your sentences easier to understand.

Remember, feedback is meant to help you grow and get better at what you're doing. So, don't be afraid to give it or receive it!

BIBLICAL REFERENCES

In the Bible, there are several passages that indirectly touch upon the concept of feedback, although the term itself may not be explicitly used. Here are a few examples:

Proverbs 27:17 (NIV): "As iron sharpens iron, so one person sharpens another." This verse suggests that through interactions with others, we can grow and improve, much like how iron tools are sharpened by friction with each other. This can be seen as a metaphor for the exchange of feedback.

Ephesians 4:15 (NIV):

> *"Instead, speaking the truth in love, we will grow to become in every respect the mature body of him who is the head, that is, Christ."*

This verse encourages honesty and love in communication. Providing feedback in a caring and constructive manner can help others mature and grow spiritually.

Colossians 3:16 (NIV):

> *"Let the message of Christ dwell among you richly as you teach and admonish one another with all wisdom through psalms, hymns, and songs from the Spirit, singing to God with gratitude in your hearts."*

This verse emphasizes the importance of teaching and admonishing one another with wisdom. Giving feedback rooted in wisdom can lead to spiritual growth and understanding.

These verses highlight the importance of communication, honesty, love, and growth in relationships, which are all elements that are integral to the process of giving and receiving feedback.

Tips for Giving Feedback:

- Be Kind: When giving feedback, remember to be nice. Say things in a friendly way so you don't hurt anyone's feelings.
- Be Specific: Instead of saying "good job," tell the person exactly what you liked. For example, say, "I really liked how you explained your ideas clearly."
- Be Helpful: Feedback is meant to help someone get better. So, try to give suggestions on how they can improve. For instance, if their writing is hard to understand, you could suggest they use simpler words.
- Be Honest: It's important, to tell the truth, but in a nice way. If you don't like something, try to say it politely and offer ideas for how it could be better.
- Be Loving: It's important that when you give feedback, you do it because you care for the other person and what they can accomplish.

Tips for Receiving Feedback:

- Listen Carefully: When someone is giving you feedback, listen carefully to what they're saying. Even if you don't agree, it's important to hear them out.
- Say Thank You: Always say thank you when someone gives you feedback. It shows that you appreciate their help, even if you don't agree with everything they say.
- Ask Questions: If you don't understand something or want more information, don't be afraid to ask questions. It's okay to ask for clarification.
- Think About It: After receiving feedback, take some time to think about it. Consider what was said and how you might use it to improve.

Remember, feedback is a way to learn and grow, so don't be afraid to give it or receive it. It's all about helping each other get better!

Discussion Questions: (Please limit to 4-5 questions that pertain to your group)

- Why is it essential to be nice and specific when giving feedback to someone?
- How do you feel when someone gives you kind and specific feedback?
- When you get feedback, why is it important to listen carefully, even if you don't agree with everything the person says?
- How can you thank someone for their feedback, even if you're not sure about it?

- How do you think giving and receiving feedback relate to the idea of learning and growing?
- Can you find any connections between feedback and getting better at something?
- Have you ever been in a situation where you received feedback that was hard to hear?
- What are some ways we can make sure we understand the feedback we receive?
- Can you share a time when you gave feedback to someone, and it helped them improve?
- Why is it important to give feedback in a caring and helpful way?
- How can we make sure our feedback shows that we want to help the other person do better?
- How can we use the idea of giving and receiving feedback in our everyday lives, like at school or with our friends and family? Can you think of any examples?

INFORMATION FOR INSTRUCTORS

Challenges:

- Fear of Offending: People may be hesitant to give feedback because they fear it will offend or upset the recipient. Similarly, individuals may struggle to receive feedback if they feel criticized or attacked, even if it is meant to be constructive.
- Lack of Trust: Without trust in the relationship, feedback may not be well-received or may not be given honestly. If people don't trust that feedback is coming from a place of genuine concern and support, they may dismiss it or become defensive.
- Poor Communication Skills: Ineffective communication skills, such as being unclear or insensitive, can hinder the giving and receiving of feedback. If feedback is not communicated clearly and respectfully, it may not be understood or accepted by the recipient.
- Cultural Differences: Cultural norms and expectations around feedback vary widely, and what may be considered appropriate in one culture may not be acceptable in another. These differences can create barriers to giving and receiving feedback effectively.
- Ego and Pride: Ego and pride can get in the way of both giving and receiving feedback. Some individuals may struggle to give feedback because they don't want to admit they don't know everything, while others may have difficulty receiving feedback because they don't want to appear weak or incompetent.
- Timing and Context: Feedback given at the wrong time or in the wrong context may not be well-received. It's essential to consider the timing and setting when giving feedback to ensure it is constructive and helpful.
- Lack of Skills or Knowledge: Sometimes, people may not have the necessary skills or knowledge to give effective feedback. Without training or experience in providing feedback, individuals may struggle to articulate their thoughts or provide actionable suggestions.

Addressing the barriers to giving and receiving feedback requires open communication, empathy, trust-building, and a willingness to learn and grow. By recognizing and overcoming these obstacles, individuals and organizations can foster a culture of constructive feedback that supports personal and professional development.

SUGGESTED GAME: FEEDBACK SPEED DATING

Give participants a piece of paper and a drawing utensil and ask them to draw a picture of an item such as an animal, a automobile, or fruit in ten minutes. Tell them to try to do a good job, but no one will be able to draw a Picasso in ten minutes with only one writing utensil.

The youth group leader sets up a rotation where each team member has time to provide positive and negative feedback about the picture to another team member. You'll need an even number of participants, so if you have an odd number in the group, the leader participates. After 30 seconds, the group leader says, "Switch," and the group rotates to the next person. The group leader facilitates the exercise, ensuring that each person can give and receive feedback.

In this exercise, teams understand the importance of clear and concise feedback. It also allows team members to practice giving and receiving feedback in a fast-paced and interactive environment. My youth group tried this, and there's a lot more laughter involved than you would assume. The activity makes receiving feedback positive.

NOTES:

DIPLOMACY
CHAPTER 29

DEFINITION

DIPLOMACY IS THE art of having good manners in dealing with people but on a bigger scale. It's about using words and negotiations instead of fights or arguments to solve problems. Just like how you might talk politely to resolve a disagreement with a friend, diplomats talk respectfully to other countries to settle conflicts or make agreements. Diplomacy is about finding common ground and making peaceful connections with others.

BIBLICAL REFERENCES

The Bible contains several passages that can be interpreted in the context of diplomacy or the art of negotiation and peacemaking. Here are a few examples:

Matthew 5:9 (NIV):

> *"Blessed are the peacemakers, for they will be called children of God."*

This verse highlights the importance of promoting peace and resolving conflicts peacefully, which is central to diplomacy.

Proverbs 15:1 (NIV):

> *"A gentle answer turns away wrath, but a harsh word stirs up anger."*

This verse emphasizes the value of diplomacy in communication and how using gentle and respectful language can help to diffuse tense situations.

Proverbs 16:7 (NIV):

> *"When the Lord takes pleasure in anyone's way, he causes their enemies to make peace with them."*

This verse suggests that diplomacy and reconciliation can be divinely influenced, implying that peaceful resolutions can be achieved through the favor of a higher power.

Romans 12:18 (NIV):

|| *"If it is possible, as far as it depends on you, live at peace with everyone."*

This verse encourages believers to seek peace and reconciliation whenever possible, highlighting the importance of diplomacy in interpersonal relationships.

These passages reflect the biblical emphasis on promoting peace, resolving conflicts, and maintaining good relationships with others, which are all fundamental aspects of diplomacy.

Developing diplomacy skills means learning how to communicate effectively, understand others, and solve problems peacefully. Here are some simple ways to improve your diplomacy skills:

- Practice Active Listening: Pay attention to what others are saying without interrupting. Show that you understand by nodding or repeating what they've said.

- Learn to Empathize: Try to see things from the other person's perspective. Understand their feelings and motivations, even if you don't agree with them.

- Stay Calm: Keep your emotions in check, even when things get heated. Take deep breaths and try to stay relaxed during disagreements.

- Use Respectful Language: Be polite and respectful in your words and actions, even if you disagree with someone. Avoid insults or aggressive behavior.

- Seek Common Ground: Look for areas where you and the other person agree and build on those points. Finding common ground can help bridge differences.

- Be Patient: Diplomacy takes time, so be patient and persistent. Don't expect to solve problems overnight.

- Practice Problem-Solving: Work together with others to find solutions to problems. Brainstorm ideas and be open to compromise.

- Learn About Different Cultures: Explore other cultures and customs to better understand and appreciate people from diverse backgrounds.

- Read Books and Watch Videos: There are plenty of resources available that can teach you more about diplomacy and how to improve your skills. Look for books, articles, and videos on the subject.

- Get Involved: Participate in activities like debate clubs or community projects where you can practice diplomacy skills in a supportive environment.

Overcoming the barriers to diplomacy requires patience, understanding, and a willingness to listen and compromise from all parties involved. By practicing these skills regularly, you can become a better diplomat and contribute to making the world a more peaceful and harmonious place.

Discussion Questions: (Please limit to 4-5 questions that pertain to your group)

- Can you think of any real-life examples where diplomacy has played a significant role in resolving conflicts or making agreements?

- How does diplomacy relate to the idea of using words and negotiations instead of fights or arguments to solve problems?

- Can you think of a time when you used diplomacy in your own life?
- How do the Biblcal verses provided emphasize the importance of promoting peace and resolving conflicts peacefully?
- What are some ways that practicing diplomacy can help improve relationships, both on a personal level and on a larger scale, such as between countries?
- How can active listening contribute to effective diplomacy?
- Why is empathy an essential skill in diplomacy?
- Can you give an example of how understanding someone else's perspective can help resolve a disagreement or conflict?
- How can staying calm and using respectful language contribute to successful diplomacy? Can you think of any situations where keeping your emotions in check helped you navigate a difficult conversation?
- Why is it important to seek common ground when practicing diplomacy? How can finding areas of agreement help build understanding and trust between parties?
- What are some ways that individuals can practice diplomacy skills in their daily lives, even if they're not involved in formal negotiations?
- How do you think diplomacy can contribute to making the world a more peaceful and harmonious place?
- What are some steps that individuals, communities, or governments can take to overcome barriers to diplomacy and promote understanding and cooperation?

INFORMATION FOR INSTRUCTORS

Barriers to diplomacy are like obstacles that make it harder for people to talk and solve problems peacefully. Here are a few examples:

- Lack of Trust: When countries don't trust each other, it's hard for them to believe what the other side is saying or to work together on common goals.
- Misunderstandings: Sometimes, countries may not understand each other's perspectives or intentions, leading to confusion and conflicts instead of cooperation.
- Cultural Differences: Different countries have different customs, traditions, and ways of doing things. These differences can sometimes lead to misunderstandings or disagreements during diplomatic negotiations.
- Historical Conflicts: Past conflicts or grievances between countries can make it difficult for them to work together in the present. Lingering resentments can get in the way of finding peaceful solutions.
- Power Imbalance: When one country is much stronger or wealthier than another, it can create an imbalance of power that makes negotiations challenging. The stronger country might try to impose its will on the weaker one, leading to tension and conflict.
- Internal Politics: Sometimes, political pressures within a country can make it harder for its leaders to engage in diplomacy. They may face opposition from within their own government or from powerful interest groups.

SUGGESTED GAME: EGG DROP

Divide your group into teams and provide each team with a raw egg, a roll of masking tape, and drinking straws. Take the teams to a location where eggs can be dropped safely at least twenty feet. Inform the teams that they have 30 minutes to develop a way to drop the eggs without the egg breaking and start the clock. The team that completes the task using only the provided materials first wins. This competition requires communication, creativity, and open decision-making for success.

Notes:

INCLUSIVENESS
CHAPTER 30

DEFINITION

INCLUSIVENESS MEANS MAKING sure that everyone feels welcome and valued, no matter their differences. It's about including people of all backgrounds, abilities, and identities and making sure they have a voice and are treated fairly. Being inclusive means accepting and respecting others for who they are and working together to create a community where everyone belongs.

BIBLICAL REFERENCES

The Bible contains several passages that emphasize inclusiveness and the importance of treating others with love, kindness, and acceptance regardless of their background or identity. Here are a few examples:

Galatians 3:28 (NIV):

> *"There is neither Jew nor Gentile, neither slave nor free, nor is there male and female, for you are all one in Christ Jesus."*

This verse highlights the idea that, in the eyes of God, all people are equal and should be treated as such.

Matthew 22:37-40 (NIV):

> *"Jesus replied: 'Love the Lord your God with all your heart and with all your soul and with all your mind.' This is the first and greatest commandment. And the second is like it: 'Love your neighbor as yourself.' All the Law and the Prophets hang on these two commandments."*

Jesus emphasizes the importance of loving others as we love ourselves, regardless of differences.

Romans 15:7 (NIV):

> *"Accept one another, then, just as Christ accepted you, in order to bring praise to God."*

This verse encourages believers to accept and welcome others just as Christ accepted them, without judgment or discrimination.

Luke 6:31 (NIV):

> *"Do to others as you would have them do to you."*

Known as the Golden Rule, this verse teaches that we should treat others with the same kindness and respect that we would want for ourselves.

These passages promote the idea of inclusiveness, acceptance, and love for all people, regardless of their differences.

Tips:

- Be Kind to Everyone: Treat everyone with respect and kindness, no matter how they look or where they come from. Being friendly and accepting can help everyone feel included.
- Listen to Others: Take the time to listen to what others have to say and try to understand their perspective. This shows that you value their thoughts and feelings.
- Learn About Different Cultures: Take the opportunity to learn about different cultures, traditions, and backgrounds. This can help you understand and appreciate people who are different from you.
- Include Everyone in Activities: When you're doing group activities or games, make sure everyone has a chance to participate. This way, everyone feels like they're part of the group.
- Stand Up Against Bullying: If you see someone being bullied or treated unfairly, speak up and stand up for them. Bullying and discrimination can make people feel excluded and hurt.
- Make New Friends: Don't just stick to hanging out with people who are exactly like you. Make an effort to make friends with people who are different from you. You might be surprised by how much you have in common!
- Be Open-Minded: Keep an open mind and be willing to learn new things. Being open to new ideas and experiences can help you grow as a person and become more inclusive.
- Include Everyone in Conversations: When you're talking with a group of people, make sure to include everyone in the conversation. This way, no one feels left out or ignored.
- Be Yourself: Finally, be true to yourself and encourage others to do the same. Embrace your own uniqueness and celebrate the differences in others. Being yourself can help create an inclusive environment where everyone feels accepted for who they are.

To be more inclusive, we need to learn about and respect each other's differences, be open to new things, and make sure that everyone feels welcome and valued.

Discussion Questions: (Please limit to 4-5 questions that pertain to your group)

- Can you give an example of a time when you felt included or excluded? How did it make you feel?
- How do the stories in the Bible teach us about being kind and accepting of others, no matter how different they may be from us?
- Why is it important to treat everyone with respect and kindness, regardless of how they look or where they come from?
- Can you think of a time when someone showed you kindness or made you feel included?
- How can we make sure that everyone feels welcome and valued in our classrooms, schools, and communities?
- What are some things we can do to include everyone?
- What does it mean to listen to others and try to understand their perspective?
- Can you think of a time when someone really listened to you and understood how you felt?
- Why is it important to stand up against bullying and discrimination?
- How can we help someone who is being treated unfairly?
- What are some ways we can include everyone in group activities or conversations?
- How can we make sure that everyone's voice is heard?
- How can being open-minded and willing to learn new things help us be more inclusive?
- Can you share a time when you learned something new about someone else's culture or background?
- Why is it important to celebrate what makes each person unique?
- How can we encourage others to be themselves?
- What can we do to promote inclusiveness in our school and community? How can we work together to make sure that everyone feels like they belong?

INFORMATION FOR INSTRUCTORS

Challenges:

- Prejudice and Discrimination: Sometimes, people unfairly judge or treat others differently because of things like their race, religion, or how much money they have. This can make it hard for everyone to feel included.
- Not Understanding Differences: Sometimes, we don't understand or know much about people who are different from us. This lack of understanding can make it tough to include them or know how to treat them.
- Being Scared of What's Different: When we're unfamiliar with something or someone, it can make us feel scared or uncomfortable. This fear can stop us from including others who seem different from us.
- Feeling Pressure to Fit In: Sometimes, we feel like we have to act or think a certain way to fit in with a group. This pressure can make it hard to include people who don't seem to fit in with what's expected.
- Unfair Rules or Systems: Sometimes, the way things are set up, like rules or how decisions

are made, can make it harder for some people to be included. This might happen if certain groups of people don't have the same opportunities as others.

- Problems with Communication: Sometimes, it's hard to understand each other because we speak different languages or have different ways of communicating. This can make it tough for everyone to feel included in conversations or activities.
- Not Realizing Our Biases: Sometimes, we don't even realize that we have unfair ideas about certain groups of people. These ideas can make it harder for us to include everyone because we might treat them differently without even knowing it.

Suggested Game: Visualization Game

The group leader reads: I'm going to ask you to visualize three scenarios. The visualization part is very important, so please close your eyes, take a deep breath, and imagine you're late to catch a flight. You rush through the airport, you make it through security, you run to the gate, you make it down the jetway, and you step on the plane. Just as they close the door behind you, the pilot steps out of the cockpit and says, "Hi." You get to your destination and go to a local restaurant. You have the best meal of your life, and at the table next to you is a couple happily celebrating their anniversary. The next morning, you go to the biggest technology conference in the world, and the CEO of this year's hottest tech startup just takes the stage to speak. Now you should have a solid picture of all of that, so open your eyes because I have some questions for you. In your mental image, was the pilot black? Was the married couple two men? Was the tech CEO on stage female?

This is called an unconscious bias. Unconscious bias is when our brains make quick judgments about people or situations without us even realizing it. These judgments are based on things like stereotypes or things we've learned from the world around us.

For example, if we see someone who looks different from us, our brain might automatically think certain things about them, even if we don't mean to. This can happen without us even noticing.

Unconscious bias can affect how we treat people without us realizing it. It might make us act differently toward someone or make assumptions about them based on things like their race, gender, or where they're from.

To fight unconscious bias, it's important to be aware of it and try to learn more about different people and cultures. This helps us treat everyone fairly and with respect, no matter what they look like or where they come from.

NOTES:

PUNCTUALITY
CHAPTER 31

DEFINITION

PUNCTUALITY MEANS BEING on time. It's about showing up when you're supposed to, finishing things when they're supposed to be done, and keeping appointments or meeting times. Being punctual shows that you're dependable and respect other people's time.

BIBLICAL REFERENCES

While the concept of punctuality as we understand it today may not be explicitly mentioned in the Bible, there are principles and teachings that emphasize the importance of being prompt and faithful in various contexts. Here are a few biblical references related to punctuality:

Ecclesiastes 3:1-8: This passage talks about the seasons and timing in life, indicating that there is a time for everything. While not directly about punctuality, it emphasizes the importance of recognizing and respecting different times and seasons.

Matthew 25:1-13 (Parable of the Ten Virgins): In this parable, Jesus tells of ten virgins waiting for the bridegroom to arrive for a wedding feast. Five of them were wise and prepared with enough oil for their lamps, while the other five were foolish and unprepared. When the bridegroom arrived unexpectedly, only the wise virgins were ready to meet him, illustrating the importance of being prepared and punctual.

Proverbs 22:29: "Do you see someone skilled in their work? They will serve before kings; they will not serve before officials of low rank." This verse highlights the value of diligence and competence in one's work, which often includes being punctual and reliable.

Colossians 4:5: "Be wise in the way you act toward outsiders; make the most of every opportunity." While not directly about punctuality, this verse encourages believers to be wise and intentional in their actions, which can include being prompt and respectful of others' time.

Overall, while the Bible may not have specific verses addressing punctuality by name, its teachings emphasize principles such as diligence, preparation, and respect for others, which are closely related to the concept of punctuality.

Improving punctuality can be easier than you think! Here are some simple tips to help you get better at being on time:

- Plan Ahead: Make a schedule for your day and figure out how long each task will take. This will help you manage your time better.
- Set Alarms: Use alarms or reminders on your phone or clock to help you stay on track and remind you when it's time to move on to the next activity.
- Get Ready Early: Try to get ready for school or events a little earlier than you think you need to. This gives you some extra time in case something unexpected comes up.
- Use a Planner or Calendar: Write down important dates and deadlines in a planner or on a calendar so you don't forget them.
- Break Tasks Into Smaller Steps: If you have a big project or assignment, break it down into smaller, manageable tasks. This can make it easier to get things done on time.
- Practice Estimating Time: Try to get better at guessing how long tasks will take you. With practice, you'll get better at planning your time effectively.
- Minimize Distractions: When you're trying to get something done, try to limit distractions like your phone, TV, or video games. This can help you stay focused and get things done faster.
- Get Enough Sleep: Make sure you're getting enough sleep at night so you're rested and ready to tackle the day. Being tired can make it harder to stay on schedule.
- Be Patient with Yourself: Remember, developing better punctuality skills takes time and practice. Don't get discouraged if you slip up now and then. Just keep trying your best!

Identifying and addressing barriers to being punctual can help individuals improve their punctuality and better manage their time. This may involve developing better time management skills, setting realistic goals and priorities, minimizing distractions, and planning ahead to anticipate potential obstacles. By following these tips and making punctuality a priority, you'll be well on your way to being more organized and on time in no time!

Discussion Questions: (Please limit to 4-5 questions that pertain to your group)

- How do you think being punctual shows respect for other people's time?
- Can you think of a situation where someone being late might cause problems for others?
- Even though the Bible may not talk about punctuality directly, how do you think the ideas of being prepared and managing your time relate to being on time?
- Why is it important to plan ahead and manage your time well?
- Can you think of any ways to minimize distractions and stay focused on tasks so you can finish them on time?
- How do you feel when you have a lot to do and not enough time to do it?
- What are some ways you can decide which tasks to do first?
- Why is it okay to make mistakes when trying to be punctual?
- How can you encourage yourself to keep trying even if you don't get it right every time?
- Can you think of any situations where being on time might be hard?
- What are some good things that can happen when you're punctual?

- How can being on time help you do well in school and in your activities?

INFORMATION FOR INSTRUCTORS

There are several common barriers to punctuality that people may face. Here are some examples:

- Poor time management skills: Difficulty in planning and organizing tasks effectively can lead to delays and missed deadlines.
- Procrastination: Putting off tasks until the last minute can result in rushing and being late.
- Distractions: Being easily distracted by phone notifications, social media, or other interruptions can cause people to lose track of time and be late.
- Underestimating time: Failing to accurately estimate how long tasks will take can lead to running late.
- Traffic and transportation issues: Delays in traffic, public transportation, or unexpected vehicle problems can cause people to arrive late despite their efforts to be on time.
- Overcommitment: Saying yes to too many obligations or trying to do too much can lead to a packed schedule and difficulty in being punctual.
- Lack of motivation: Not seeing the importance of being on time or feeling indifferent towards punctuality can result in a lack of effort to arrive promptly.
- Poor sleep habits: Inadequate sleep or difficulty waking up in the morning can make it challenging to get ready and leave on time.
- External factors: Family responsibilities, health issues, or emergencies may arise unexpectedly, making it difficult to adhere to a punctual schedule.

SUGGESTED GAME: WHAT I DID YESTERDAY.

This game requires only a piece of paper, a writing utensil for each person, and a timer. Using the timer, give the players ten minutes. The players write down everything they did yesterday as quickly as possible. The person with the longest list is the winner.

NOTES:

EMOTIONAL AWARENESS
CHAPTER 32

DEFINITION

EMOTIONAL AWARENESS MEANS understanding and recognizing your own feelings and the feelings of others. It's like having a map of your emotions, knowing what they are and why you feel them. Being emotionally aware helps you make better choices in how you react to situations and how you communicate with others. It's important because it helps you understand yourself better and build stronger relationships with people around you.

BIBLICAL REFERENCES:

In the Bible, there are numerous references to emotions and the importance of understanding them.

Proverbs 14:29 (NIV):

> *"Whoever is patient has great understanding, but one who is quick-tempered displays folly."*

This verse highlights the importance of patience and self-control in managing emotions.

Ephesians 4:26-27 (NIV):

> *"In your anger do not sin: Do not let the sun go down while you are still angry, and do not give the devil a foothold."*

This verse acknowledges the natural experience of anger but advises against letting it control one's actions and urges for resolution before the day ends.

Galatians 5:22-23 (NIV):

> *"But the fruit of the Spirit is love, joy, peace, forbearance, kindness, goodness, faithfulness, gentleness and self-control. Against such things, there is no law."*

Here, emotional awareness is linked to the fruit of the Spirit, emphasizing qualities such as self-control and peace.

Colossians 3:12-13 (NIV):

> *"Therefore, as God's chosen people, holy and dearly loved, clothe yourselves with compassion, kindness, humility, gentleness and patience. Bear with each other and forgive one another if any of you has a grievance against someone. Forgive as the Lord forgave you."*

This passage highlights the importance of empathy, forgiveness, and understanding in interpersonal relationships.

These verses emphasize the significance of understanding and managing emotions in alignment with biblical principles. They encourage believers to cultivate virtues such as patience, self-control, compassion, and forgiveness, which are essential aspects of emotional awareness and regulation.

Here are some tips on how to be more emotionally aware:

- Pay Attention to Your Feelings: Take time to notice how you're feeling throughout the day. Try to label your emotions with words like "happy," "sad," or "frustrated."
- Practice Self-Reflection: Spend a few minutes each day reflecting on your emotions. Ask yourself why you might be feeling a certain way and how those feelings might be influencing your thoughts and actions.
- Listen to Others: Pay attention to the emotions of the people around you. Look for cues like facial expressions, tone of voice, and body language to understand how they might be feeling.
- Ask Questions: If you're unsure about someone's emotions, don't be afraid to ask. Simple questions like "How are you feeling?" or "Is everything okay?" can show that you care and help you better understand their perspective.
- Practice Empathy: Try to imagine what it would be like to be in someone else's shoes. Consider how you would feel if you were experiencing the same situation they are.
- Express Yourself: Don't be afraid to share your own emotions with others. Being open and honest about how you're feeling can help deepen your connections with those around you.
- Seek Support: If you're struggling with your emotions, don't hesitate to reach out for help. Talk to a trusted friend, family member, or counselor who can offer support and guidance.

It's important to recognize the barriers of being emotionally aware so you can work on understanding and accepting your emotions better. Remember, being emotionally aware takes practice, so be patient with yourself as you work on developing this skill.

Discussion Questions: (Please limit to 4-5 questions that pertain to your group)

- Can you give an example of a time when you noticed your own feelings or someone else's feelings?
- How can understanding your own emotions help you make better choices in how you react to different situations?

- Can you think of a time when being aware of your feelings helped you handle a problem?
- How do the Bible verses we talked about relate to the idea of understanding emotions?
- Can you find any connections between these teachings and the importance of managing feelings in a good way?
- Why do you think it's important to pay attention to how you're feeling and think about why you feel that way?
- How can understanding your emotions help you have a better day?
- Can you think of any ways to show empathy, which means understanding and sharing the feelings of others?
- How do you think being empathetic can help you get along better with your friends and family?
- Why is it important to talk about your own feelings and listen when others share theirs?
- How can being open about how you feel help you and the people around you?
- What are some things you can do every day to practice being aware of your emotions?
- Can you think of any strategies for calming down when you feel upset or angry?
- How can talking to someone you trust, like a friend or family member, help you understand your feelings better?
- Can you share a time when talking to someone made you feel better when you were upset?
- What are some things that might make it hard to understand how you're feeling?
- How do you think being aware of your emotions can help you have a happier and healthier life?
- What are some goals you can set for yourself to keep working on understanding your feelings better?

Information for Instructors

Challenges:

Barriers to understanding your emotions can be things that make it hard for you to know how you're feeling or why.

- Ignoring Feelings: Sometimes, we pretend our emotions aren't there or try to push them away instead of facing them.
- Not Knowing Emotion Words: If you don't have words to describe how you're feeling, it's tough to understand and express those emotions.
- Cultural Beliefs: Some cultures or communities might teach that certain emotions are bad or should be hidden, which can make it hard to be aware of and accept those feelings.
- Past Hurts: If you've been hurt before, it might make you not want to feel those emotions again, so you try to block them out.
- Fear of Being Judged: You might worry about what others will think if you show your emotions, so you keep them to yourself.

- Being Too Busy: With lots of things going on, it's easy to ignore your feelings or not even notice them.
- Thinking Too Much: Instead of feeling your emotions, you might try to analyze them too much or explain them away, which can make it hard to understand what you're really feeling.

SUGGESTED GAME: EMOTIONAL CHARADES

Make a list of emotions and place them into a bowl. The game is played as a regular charades game, but the participants will act out emotions for others to guess.

Here's a partial list to get you started:

1. Happiness
2. Sadness
3. Anger
4. Fear
5. Surprise
6. Disgust
7. Excitement
8. Anxiety
9. Contentment
10. Frustration
11. Love
12. Jealousy
13. Guilt
14. Shame
15. Pride
16. Gratitude
17. Compassion
18. Confusion
19. Loneliness
20. Envy

NOTES:

MENTORSHIP
CHAPTER 33

DEFINITION

MENTORSHIP IS WHEN someone older and more experienced helps and guides someone younger or less experienced. It's like having a wise friend or advisor who supports you, gives you advice, and helps you learn and grow. They're there to answer questions, give encouragement, and share their knowledge to help you succeed and reach your goals.

BIBLICAL REFERENCES

While the term "mentorship" may not be explicitly used in the Bible, there are several instances of mentorship-like relationships and principles that can be found throughout the Scriptures:

Elijah and Elisha: In 1 Kings 19, we see the prophet Elijah being instructed by God to anoint Elisha as his successor. Elisha then becomes Elijah's disciple, following him closely, learning from him, and eventually inheriting his mantle as a prophet.

Moses and Joshua: Moses served as a mentor to Joshua, guiding and preparing him to lead the Israelites after Moses' death. In Deuteronomy 31:7-8, Moses publicly commissions Joshua before the people, encouraging him to be strong and courageous.

Paul and Timothy: The apostle Paul had a close mentorship relationship with Timothy, whom he referred to as his "son in the faith" (1 Timothy 1:2). Paul provided guidance, encouragement, and instruction to Timothy as he ministered to the early Christian communities.

Jesus and His Disciples: Jesus served as a mentor to his disciples, teaching them through both his words and actions. He invested time in their development, providing spiritual guidance and equipping them to carry on his ministry after his departure.

Naomi and Ruth: In the book of Ruth, we see Naomi serving as a mentor to her daughter-in-law Ruth, guiding her and providing wisdom as Ruth navigates her new life in a foreign land.

These examples illustrate the importance of mentoring relationships in the Bible, where individuals with more experience and wisdom invest in and guide those who are younger or less experienced. They emphasize the value of passing on knowledge, skills, and faith from one generation to the next, embodying principles of discipleship, guidance, and encouragement.

Tips on being a mentor:

- Be Open and Friendly: Try to be open and friendly with your mentor or mentee. Being approachable and kind makes it easier to talk and share ideas.
- Listen Carefully: Listen carefully when your mentor or mentee is talking. It shows that you care about what they have to say and helps you understand each other better.
- Ask Questions: Don't be afraid to ask questions if you're not sure about something. Asking questions is a great way to learn and get to know each other better.
- Share Your Ideas: Share your thoughts and ideas with your mentor or mentee. They can offer advice and help you see things from different perspectives.
- Set Goals Together: Work together to set goals for your mentorship. It gives you something to work towards and helps you stay focused.
- Be Patient: Be patient with yourself and each other. Building a strong mentorship takes time, so don't get discouraged if things don't happen right away.
- Be Respectful: Treat your mentor or mentee with respect. It's important to be polite and considerate of each other's feelings.
- Celebrate Successes: Celebrate your achievements together, no matter how big or small. It's a great way to stay motivated and build confidence.
- Stay Committed: Make a commitment to each other to stick with your mentorship. It shows that you value each other's time and effort.
- Have Fun: Most importantly, have fun with your mentorship! Enjoy spending time together, learning new things, and building a strong relationship.

Being a mentor or mentee is important because it helps everyone learn and grow. Being a mentor means you get to share your knowledge and experience with someone eager to learn from you. Being a mentee means you get guidance and support from someone who's been there before. It's like having a friend to help you navigate through life's ups and downs. Plus, mentoring builds strong connections and can open up new opportunities for everyone involved. So whether you're offering guidance or seeking it, being part of a mentoring relationship can make a big difference in your life.

Discussion Questions: (Please limit to 4-5 questions that pertain to your group)

- Can you give an example of someone who helps and guides you, like a coach or an older sibling?
- How do you think having a mentor is like having a wise friend?
- Can you think of a time when someone older gave you good advice or support?
- Can you find any stories in the Bible where someone helps and guides another person? How are these stories similar to having a mentor today?
- Why is it important to have someone to help you and give you advice?
- How can having a mentor make it easier to achieve your goals?

- What are some things a good mentor might do to help you learn and grow?
- Can you think of qualities you'd like in a mentor, like being patient or a good listener?
- How do you think listening carefully and asking questions can help you learn from a mentor?
- Can you share an example of a time when you learned something new by asking questions?
- Why is it important to be respectful and patient when working with a mentor?
- How can showing respect and being patient help you build a strong relationship with your mentor?
- What are some goals you might set with your mentor?
- How can working towards these goals together help you both learn and improve?
- How can you celebrate successes with your mentor? Why is it important to acknowledge and celebrate your achievements together?
- How do you think having a mentor can help both you and the mentor?
- Can you share a time when someone helped you, and it made a big difference in your life?

INFORMATION FOR INSTRUCTORS

Challenges:

- Not Enough Time: Sometimes, both the mentor and the person being mentored (called the mentee) are too busy with other things to spend time together and learn from each other.
- Different Expectations: If the mentor and the mentee want different things from the mentorship, it can make it hard for them to work together and understand each other.
- Not Talking Enough: Good communication, or talking openly and honestly, is really important in mentorship. If the mentor and mentee don't talk enough or have trouble sharing their thoughts and feelings, it can make the mentorship less effective.
- Feeling Scared to Share: Sometimes, people feel nervous about sharing their thoughts and feelings with each other, especially if they don't know each other very well. This can make it hard to build trust and have a strong mentorship.
- Power Differences: If one person in the mentorship has more authority or experience than the other, it can make the relationship feel unbalanced and stop them from understanding each other well.
- Not Finding the Right Mentor: It can be tough to find someone who is a good fit to be a mentor, especially if there aren't many people available to choose from.
- Cultural or Age Differences: If the mentor and mentee come from different backgrounds or generations, they might have a hard time understanding each other because they see things differently.
- Being Far Apart: Sometimes, if the mentor and mentee live far away from each other or can't meet in person, it can make it hard to build a close mentorship relationship.
- Having Too Many Other Things to Do: Sometimes, both the mentor and the mentee have

so many other things going on in their lives that they don't have enough time to focus on their mentorship.

- Not Enough Help from Others: If the school or community doesn't have programs or support for mentorship, it can be harder for people to find mentors and make their mentorships work.

SUGGESTED GAME: THE QUESTIONS GAME

Pair your team up and ask the first question. Give them time to give the answer to each other, and then ask them to change partners before you ask the next question. These are meant to open communication and be fun. You may hear a lot of laughter. After the game, they can talk about it.

1. What person, living or dead, would you most want to meet and why?
2. What is the most daredevil thing you've ever done, and how was that experience?
3. What do you want to be remembered for when you die?
4. What cartoon character is most like you?
5. What question do you wish people would ask you?
6. What day in your life would you like to relive?
7. What is your superpower?
8. What would you do if you knew you couldn't fail?
9. If you could be a character in any movie, what character and what movie would it be?
10. A genie grants you one wish; what do you wish for?
11. What would you title your biography?

NOTES:

Moral Courage
Chapter 34

Definition

THE LEADERSHIP QUALITY that compels leaders to stand up for what's right is often referred to as moral courage or ethical fortitude. This trait involves a strong sense of integrity, conviction, and willingness to take a stand, even when faced with opposition, adversity, or potential personal risk. Leaders with moral courage prioritize principles and values over self-interest or popular opinion, demonstrating a commitment to ethical behavior and doing what they believe is right, regardless of the consequences. They inspire trust and respect among their followers, fostering a culture of honesty, fairness, and accountability within their organizations or communities.

Biblical References

Joshua 1:9 (NIV):

> *"Have I not commanded you? Be strong and courageous. Do not be afraid; do not be discouraged, for the Lord your God will be with you wherever you go."*

This verse encourages individuals to exhibit courage and strength, knowing that God is always present to support them.

Proverbs 28:1 (NIV):

> *"The wicked flee though no one pursues, but the righteous are as bold as a lion."*

This verse contrasts the behavior of the wicked, who are cowardly, with the righteous, who demonstrate boldness and courage.

1 Corinthians 16:13 (NIV):

> *"Be on your guard; stand firm in the faith; be courageous; be strong."*

This verse urges believers to stand firm in their faith and to be courageous and strong in the face of challenges.

Acts 4:19-20 (NIV):

> *"But Peter and John replied, 'Which is right in God's eyes: to listen to you, or to him? You be the judges! As for us, we cannot help speaking about what we have seen and heard.'"*

This passage illustrates the apostles' determination to obey God rather than human authorities, demonstrating moral courage in the proclamation of their beliefs.

2 Timothy 1:7 (NIV):

> *"For the Spirit God gave us does not make us timid, but gives us power, love and self-discipline."*

This verse emphasizes that God provides the strength and courage needed to overcome fear and stand up for what is right.

These biblical references highlight the importance of moral courage in the lives of believers, encouraging them to trust in God's support as they uphold their convictions and principles.

Tips:

- Know Your Values: Take some time to think about what's important to you. Consider what you believe is right and wrong. Knowing your values will help you stand up for what you believe in.
- Educate Yourself: Learn about different issues and perspectives. The more you know, the better equipped you'll be to make informed decisions and take a stand on important issues.
- Practice Empathy: Try to understand how others might feel in different situations. Putting yourself in someone else's shoes can help you empathize with them and find the courage to stand up for them if they're being treated unfairly.
- Start Small: You don't have to take on huge challenges all at once. Start by speaking up in smaller situations where you see something wrong. As you build confidence, you'll be better prepared to tackle bigger issues.
- Find Support: Surround yourself with people who share your values and beliefs. Having friends, family, or mentors who support you can give you the strength and encouragement you need to be morally courageous.
- Stay Positive: It's easy to feel discouraged but try to stay positive and focus on making a difference. Remember that even small acts of courage can have a big impact.
- Take Risks: Being morally courageous often means taking risks, but it's important to weigh the risks against the potential benefits. Sometimes, doing what's right is worth taking a chance.
- Be Persistent: Change doesn't happen overnight, so be patient and persistent. Keep speaking up and standing up for what you believe in, even if progress is slow.
- Reflect on Your Actions: Take time to reflect on your choices and actions. Think about what went well and what you could improve on. Learning from your experiences will help you grow and become even more morally courageous.

The barriers listed can make it difficult for individuals to develop moral courage, but with support, guidance, and practice, people can overcome them and find the strength to do what's right. By following these tips and staying true to your values, you can become more morally courageous and make a positive impact on the world around you.

Discussion Questions: (Please limit to 4-5 questions that pertain to your group)

- Can you give an example of Moral Courage from your own life or from history or literature?
- How do you think moral courage relates to leadership?
- Do you believe that having a strong sense of integrity and conviction is important for leaders?
- In what ways do you think fear of consequences can prevent people from standing up for what's right?
- Can you think of any examples where fear of consequences influenced someone's decision-making?
- Do you think peer pressure can be a barrier to moral courage?
- How can individuals resist peer pressure and stay true to their values?
- Why do you think it's important for individuals to have support from friends, family, or community when trying to be morally courageous?
- How can having support impact someone's ability to stand up for what's right?
- Can you think of any instances where reflection has helped you or someone else become more morally courageous?

INFORMATION FOR INSTRUCTORS

Challenges:
- Fear of Consequences: Many people are afraid of what might happen if they stand up for what's right. They worry about being punished, criticized, or rejected by others.
- Peer Pressure: Sometimes, people feel pressured to go along with the crowd, even if they know it's wrong. They're afraid of being judged or excluded if they don't follow what everyone else is doing.
- Lack of Confidence: Some people doubt themselves and their ability to make a difference. They may feel unsure about speaking up or taking action, especially if they feel alone in their beliefs.
- Uncertainty: It can be hard to know what the right thing to do is in certain situations. People might struggle to understand their own values or worry about making the wrong decision.
- Social Norms: Society often has unwritten rules about how people should behave. These norms can make it difficult for individuals to challenge the status quo or speak out against injustices.
- Personal Risk: Standing up for what's right can sometimes involve personal risks, such as

facing retaliation or losing relationships or opportunities. Many people are reluctant to take these risks.

- Lack of Support: Without support from friends, family, or community, it can be hard for individuals to find the strength to act courageously. Feeling isolated or alone in their beliefs can make it even more challenging to take a stand.

SUGGESTED GAME: COURAGE TAG

Needed: Small and large bean bags and a safety zone made of painter's tape or chalk.

Please read to your group:

This game is all about teamwork and taking risks to help each other out. Imagine you're living in a place where there are scary monsters lurking around. In the game, most of the players are "runners," trying to avoid being caught by the monster, who is a "chaser."

Each runner wears a small bean bag on their head, while the chaser wears a bigger one. The chaser's job is to tag the runners and freeze them by knocking off their bean bags. But here's the twist: if a runner gets frozen, they can only be unfrozen by another runner putting their bean bag back on.

There's a safety zone where runners can hide from the monster, but they also need to come out and rescue their frozen friends. If the monster reaches the home base, everyone in the safety zone has to leave it immediately.

The game encourages bravery because runners have to risk getting caught themselves to help others. If there are not enough runners getting frozen, you can add more monsters to make it more challenging. And if all the runners get frozen, one of the monsters becomes a runner to help out.

It's a fun way to learn about teamwork, taking risks, and helping each other out, all while playing together!

NOTES:

COLLABORATION
CHAPTER 35

DEFINITION

COLLABORATION MEANS WORKING together with other people to achieve a common goal or complete a task. It's like when you and your friends join forces to solve a problem, finish a project, or create something cool. It's about sharing ideas, helping each other out, and combining everyone's strengths to make things happen. Collaboration is all about teamwork and supporting each other to get things done better and faster than you could alone.

BIBLICAL REFERENCES

In the Bible, there are several instances where collaboration, teamwork, or cooperation among individuals or groups are highlighted. Here are a few examples:

Exodus 18:13-27 - This passage describes how Moses' father-in-law, Jethro, advised him to appoint leaders of tens, fifties, hundreds, and thousands to help him judge the people and settle disputes. This delegation of responsibilities enabled collaboration and made the task more manageable.

Ecclesiastes 4:9-12 - This passage emphasizes the strength of collaboration and support, stating, "Two are better than one because they have a good return for their labor... Though one may be overpowered, two can defend themselves. A cord of three strands is not quickly broken."

Acts 2:42-47 - In this section, the early Christian community is described as being unified in purpose and sharing everything they had. They collaborated in worship, fellowship, and in meeting each other's needs.

1 Corinthians 12:12-27 - This passage compares the church to a body, emphasizing the importance of different parts working together for the overall well-being of the body. Just as the parts of the body collaborate to function effectively, members of the church are encouraged to collaborate and support one another.

These are just a few examples of biblical references to collaboration, teamwork, and cooperation found throughout the Bible.

Tips:

Encouraging collaboration means helping people work together better. Here are some simple ways to do it:

- Talk and Listen: Make sure everyone feels comfortable sharing ideas and listening to each other.
- Know What You're Doing: Make sure everyone understands what they're supposed to be doing and why.
- Learn New Skills: Teach everyone the skills they need to work well with others.
- Trust Each Other: Be reliable and honest so everyone feels safe working together.
- Say Thanks: Recognize when people work together well and celebrate it.
- Work Together: Show everyone how to work as a team by doing it yourself.
- Include Everyone: Make sure everyone feels welcome and respected, no matter who they are.
- Give What You Need: Make sure everyone has what they need to work together, like time, space, and tools.
- Have Fun Together: Do activities that help everyone get along and have fun while working together.

Understanding and overcoming these barriers can help make collaboration smoother and more successful. Collaboration brings people together, helps them learn from each other, and gets things done more efficiently.

Discussion Questions: (Please limit to 4-5 questions that pertain to your group)

- Can you think of any personal experiences where you collaborated with others to achieve a goal or complete a task?
- Have you ever experienced any of the barriers listed in a group project or teamwork situation?
- Can you provide examples of how clear communication can enhance collaboration, and how a lack of communication can hinder it?
- Reflecting on your own experiences, do you believe that having a shared goal is essential for successful collaboration?
- Can you think of any examples where differing goals hindered collaboration?
- Can you think of any examples where poor leadership negatively affected collaboration?
- How can celebrating successes and recognizing contributions promote a collaborative environment?
- Can you share any experiences where acknowledgment of teamwork enhanced motivation and productivity within a group?
- Think about the importance of inclusivity and diversity in collaboration. How can ensuring that everyone feels welcome and respected contribute to better collaboration?
- Can you provide examples of how diverse perspectives can enrich collaboration and lead to better outcomes?

INFORMATION FOR INSTRUCTORS

Challenges:

- Lack of Communication: When people don't talk to each other or share their ideas clearly, it's hard to collaborate because everyone might end up doing their own thing.
- Conflict: If there are disagreements or fights between people, it makes it tough to work together. It's like having a big roadblock in the way of getting things done.
- Trust Issues: Collaboration works best when people trust each other. If someone feels like they can't rely on others or that their ideas won't be respected, they might not want to collaborate.
- Different Goals: Sometimes, people have different ideas about what they want to achieve. If everyone isn't on the same page about the goal, it's hard to work together effectively.
- Lack of Resources: If there aren't enough tools, time, or support to work together, collaboration becomes really difficult. It's like trying to build a house without any bricks or tools.
- Lack of Skills: If people don't have the right skills or knowledge for the task at hand, it can be challenging to collaborate effectively. It's like trying to play a game without knowing the rules.
- Leadership Issues: When there isn't clear leadership or direction, collaboration can become chaotic. It's like trying to drive a car without someone to steer.

SUGGESTED GAME: PLAN A MEAL TOGETHER

Your meeting should be including time to eat together. This time, let the members take the lead. Encourage them to plan and cook the next meal together using collaboration and use the opportunity to invite others to attend a youth group meeting. Depending on the size of your church and youth group, this may be a time when the youth group can help with an after-service luncheon for the congregation.

Remind them that they must collaborate to develop a menu, bring anything they need to make the meal and be in charge of cleanup after the meal, which includes taking out the trash. Encourage them to make a detailed list of everything they will need and do.

Notes:

ETHICS
CHAPTER 36

DEFINITION

ETHICS IS ABOUT figuring out what's right and wrong in how we treat each other and the world around us. It's like having a set of rules or guidelines that help us make good decisions and be fair to everyone. It's about being honest, kind, and respectful to others and thinking about how our actions affect others and our environment.

BIBLICAL REFERENCES

The Bible contains numerous references to ethics, moral principles, and guidance on how to live a good and righteous life. Here are some examples:

The Ten Commandments (Exodus 20:1-17): These commandments, given by God to Moses, outline fundamental ethical principles such as worshiping only one God, respecting parents, not stealing, not killing, and not lying.

The Golden Rule (Matthew 7:12):

> *"So whatever you wish that others would do to you, do also to them, for this is the Law and the Prophets."*

This verse teaches the importance of treating others with kindness and fairness, a core principle of ethics.

The Parable of the Good Samaritan (Luke 10:25-37): This story illustrates the importance of showing compassion and helping those in need, regardless of differences or prejudices.

Love Your Neighbor as Yourself (Mark 12:31): Jesus teaches that loving one's neighbor as oneself is one of the greatest commandments, emphasizing the importance of empathy, compassion, and kindness towards others.

The Sermon on the Mount (Matthew 5-7): In this sermon, Jesus provides ethical teachings on various topics, including anger, adultery, forgiveness, and loving one's enemies, promoting a life of humility, mercy, and righteousness.

These are just a few examples, as the Bible contains many more teachings and stories that address ethical behavior and moral principles.

Tips to being more ethical:

- Be honest: Always tell the truth, even when it's hard.
- Treat others kindly: Be nice to people and try to understand how they feel.
- Respect differences: Everyone is different, and that's okay. Treat people with respect, even if they're not like you.
- Think before you act: Before doing something, ask yourself if it's the right thing to do and if it could hurt someone.
- Stand up for what's right: If you see someone being treated unfairly or something wrong happening, speak up and try to help.
- Take responsibility: If you make a mistake, admit it and try to fix it. Don't blame others for your actions.
- Consider consequences: Think about how your actions might affect others and the world around you before you do them.
- Follow rules and laws: Laws and rules are there to keep everyone safe and treated fairly. Follow them.
- Listen to your conscience: If something feels wrong, it probably is. Trust your instincts.
- Learn from others: Pay attention to how others behave ethically and try to follow their example.

Being ethical means doing what's right, even when it's not easy. It's about being a good person and treating others with kindness and fairness. To do the right thing, you have to be brave, think about how your actions affect others, and remember what's important to you. Sometimes, it also helps to talk to someone you trust for advice.

Discussion Questions: (Please limit to 4-5 questions that pertain to your group)

- Can you share any personal experiences or examples of battling the ethical barriers mentioned?
- Why is it important to consider the consequences of our actions before we act, as mentioned in the tips section?
- Can you think of any situation in your life where considering consequences might have changed the outcome?
- How can listening to your conscience help you make ethical decisions?
- Can you think of a time when your conscience guided you to do the right thing?
- What role do rules and laws play in ethical behavior?
- Do you think it's possible to be ethical even if something isn't explicitly against the law?
- Can you think of any role models or examples of ethical behavior in your life or in history?

INFORMATION FOR INSTRUCTORS

Challenges:

- Thinking only about yourself: Sometimes, people care more about what they want than what's right. They might do things like lie, cheat, or use others to get what they want.
- Feeling pressure from friends: Friends or groups might push you to do things you know are wrong just to fit in or be accepted.
- Not knowing what's right: Sometimes, people don't understand that their actions can hurt others. They might not realize they're doing something wrong.
- Different cultures: In different places, what's okay to do can be different. This can make it hard to know what's right and wrong when people from different cultures interact.
- Feeling pressure from authority: Sometimes, bosses or leaders might push people to do things that aren't right because they want to reach certain goals or please someone in charge.
- Being scared of getting in trouble: Fear of punishment can stop people from doing the right thing, especially if they see others getting away with doing wrong things.
- Complicated situations: Some problems have no easy solution. When there are many different factors to consider, it can be hard to know what the right thing to do is.

SUGGESTED GAME: BEACH BALL TOSS

Supplies: Inflatable beach ball, permanent marker

Process: Blow up an inflatable beach ball. Write various questions (examples provided below) all over the beach ball. Ask students to toss the ball, making sure each person gets a turn. When they catch the ball, each student will answer the question under their left thumb. Emphasize the importance of respecting each other's answers. Feel free to encourage group discussion to lengthen the activity.

Sample Ethics-Related Questions:

- How would you describe respect?
- What makes you feel respected?
- What comes to mind when you think of the word integrity?
- Who would you describe as someone with integrity, and why?
- In what ways are you accountable in your daily life?
- How do you hold yourself accountable?
- Why does transparency matter?
- Describe something in your community you feel is unfair. How would you change it?
- Is it ever okay to lie?

NOTES:

Drive or Passion
Chapter 37

Definition

PASSION OR DRIVE is a strong feeling or desire inside you that motivates you to pursue something you love or believe in. It's like a fire that pushes you to work hard, overcome challenges, and keep going even when things get tough. Whether it's a hobby, a goal, or a cause you care about deeply, passion or drive gives you the energy and determination to follow your dreams and make a difference in your life and the world around you.

Biblical References

Colossians 3:23-24 (NIV):

> *"Whatever you do, work at it with all your heart, as working for the Lord, not for human masters, since you know that you will receive an inheritance from the Lord as a reward. It is the Lord Christ you are serving."*

This verse emphasizes the importance of putting your whole heart and effort into your work, which can be seen as a form of drive or passion.

Proverbs 16:3 (NIV):

> *"Commit to the Lord whatever you do, and he will establish your plans."*

This verse suggests that dedication and commitment to your endeavors, guided by faith, can lead to success and fulfillment, indicating a sense of drive.

Romans 12:11 (NIV):

> *"Never be lacking in zeal, but keep your spiritual fervor, serving the Lord."*

This verse encourages believers to maintain enthusiasm and passion in their service to God, which can translate to other aspects of life as well.

Philippians 3:14 (NIV):

> *"I press on toward the goal to win the prize for which God has called me heavenward in Christ Jesus."*

This verse speaks to perseverance and determination in pursuing goals, reflecting a strong sense of drive and purpose.

These verses, among others in the Bible, highlight the importance of commitment, diligence, and enthusiasm in various aspects of life, reflecting the concept of drive or passion.

Tips:
- Explore Different Activities: Try out different hobbies, sports, arts, or clubs to see what you enjoy. Don't be afraid to experiment and see what feels right for you.
- Pay Attention to What Excites You: Notice the activities or subjects that make you feel excited or curious. Your passion is often connected to what makes you feel happy and engaged.
- Think About Your Strengths: Consider what you're good at or what comes naturally to you. Your passion might be related to your talents or skills.
- Reflect on Your Values: Think about the things that are important to you and what you care about. Your passion could align with your values and beliefs.
- Try New Things With Friends: Sometimes, trying new things with friends can make the experience more enjoyable and help you discover shared interests.
- Don't Rush It: Finding your passion can take time, so be patient with yourself. Keep exploring and trying new things until you find something that truly resonates with you.
- Listen to Your Heart: Pay attention to your feelings and intuition. Your passion is often something that feels right deep inside you.
- Stay Open-Minded: Be open to new experiences and opportunities. Your passion might be something you never expected.
- Ask for Guidance: Don't hesitate to seek advice from teachers, family members, or mentors. They can offer insights and support as you explore your interests.
- Have Fun: Above all, remember that finding your passion should be fun and enjoyable. Embrace the journey and have fun along the way!

Recognizing these barriers and finding ways to overcome them can help us become more driven and motivated to pursue our passions and achieve our dreams. You were created with a passion and a purpose. Finding what drives you and a passion for a goal is part of life's journey. If you haven't found yours yet, it's ok. Think of the journey as a fun road trip you've taken with friends.

Discussion Questions: (Please limit to 4-5 questions that pertain to your group)
- Why is it important to have a passion or drive in pursuing our goals?
- Can you relate to any of these barriers to being driven in your own life?
- Can you think of any personal strategies or examples of overcoming the barriers to being driven?

- Which tip do you find most helpful to finding your passion, and why?
- Have you ever experienced a time when you felt particularly driven or passionate about something? What was it, and what motivated you?
- How do you think having a passion or drive can positively impact your life and the lives of those around you?
- Do you think it's important to seek guidance from others when exploring our passions? Why or why not?
- In your opinion, what role does perseverance play in developing and maintaining passion or drive?

Information for Instructors

Sometimes, there are things that can get in the way of being motivated and driven towards our goals. These things are called barriers. They can be like obstacles that make it hard for us to move forward and can include:

- Fear: Feeling afraid of failure or criticism can hold us back from pursuing our passions. Fear can make us doubt ourselves and stop us from taking risks.
- Lack of Confidence: Not believing in ourselves or our abilities can make it difficult to feel motivated. When we don't feel confident, we may not even try to reach our goals.
- Distractions: Things like social media, video games, or other activities can distract us from focusing on our goals. These distractions can make it hard to stay motivated and stay on track.
- Negative Influences: People who are negative or discouraging can affect our motivation. If we're surrounded by people who don't support our goals, it can be hard to stay driven.
- Lack of Support: Sometimes, we need support from others to help us stay motivated. If we don't have support from friends, family, or teachers, it can be challenging to keep pushing forward.
- Procrastination: Putting off tasks or waiting until the last minute can prevent us from reaching our full potential. Procrastination can make it hard to stay driven because we're not taking action towards our goals.

Suggested Game: The question game

As a group, ask your participants to answer these ten questions one at a time. Allow each participant to speak and encourage positive responses. Have your group write down their own answers as they talk about it so they can have a list to refer to later.

1. As a kid, I dreamed of being a _____.
2. I can't pass up a book or a movie about _____.
3. If I played hooky from school for a week, I'd spend my time _____.
4. Most people don't know this about me, but I really enjoy _____.

5. I am the go-to person when my friends need help with _____.

6. If I could star in my own How-to TV show, it would be about _____.

7. If I were to make someone a homemade gift, it would involve _____.

8. I've tried it only once or twice, but I really enjoy _____.

9. The closest thing I've ever experienced to a runner's high is _____.

10. If I won first prize in a talent show, it would be for _____.

Referring to the list made by the participants, have them look for a common link between all of the answers to the questions.

NOTES:

CREATIVITY AND INNOVATION
CHAPTER 38

DEFINITION

CREATIVITY IS WHEN you use your imagination to come up with new and original ideas or ways to make something better. Innovation is when you take those creative ideas and turn them into something real and useful.

BIBLICAL REFERENCES

In the Bible, there are several instances where innovation or creative problem-solving is demonstrated. Here are a few examples:

Noah's Ark (Genesis 6-9): In the story of Noah's Ark, God instructs Noah to build a huge boat to save his family and animals from a catastrophic flood. This required innovation in construction, as it was likely the first time such a massive vessel had been built.

The Tower of Babel (Genesis 11:1-9): Although the outcome of this story is not positive, the people's creativity and intention to build a tower reaching to the heavens demonstrates their innovative spirit and ambition to achieve great feats.

Bezalel and Oholiab (Exodus 31:1-11): These two men were chosen by God to oversee the construction of the Tabernacle, a portable sanctuary for worship. They were filled with the Spirit of God and given wisdom, understanding, and skills in all kinds of crafts to innovate and create the intricate and beautiful components of the Tabernacle.

David's Sling (1 Samuel 17): When David faced the giant Goliath, he used an unconventional weapon—a sling—to defeat him. David's choice of weapon and his skill in using it effectively against a much larger opponent demonstrate innovative thinking and courage.

Solomon's Temple (1 Kings 6): King Solomon's construction of the Temple in Jerusalem required innovative architectural and engineering solutions to create a grand and sacred space for worship.

These examples from the Bible illustrate instances where individuals or groups used creative problem-solving and innovation to overcome challenges, fulfill divine instructions, or achieve significant goals.

Tips:

- Explore new experiences: Try new activities, visit new places, or learn about different cultures. Experiencing new things can spark creativity and inspire new ideas.
- Keep an open mind: Be willing to consider different perspectives and ideas, even if they seem unusual or unconventional.
- Practice brainstorming: Set aside time to brainstorm ideas without judging or censoring yourself. Quantity over quality at first can lead to breakthroughs later on.
- Take breaks: Sometimes, stepping away from a problem or task can give your mind the space it needs to come up with fresh ideas. Take regular breaks and engage in activities that relax and recharge you.
- Collaborate with others: Working with people from diverse backgrounds and skill sets can bring new insights and perspectives to your work, leading to more innovative solutions.
- Embrace failure: See failure as an opportunity to learn and grow rather than something to be avoided at all costs. Some of the most innovative ideas come from taking risks and learning from mistakes.
- Ask questions: Challenge assumptions and ask why things are done a certain way. This can help uncover new opportunities for improvement or innovation.
- Keep a creative journal: Write down your ideas, observations, and inspirations regularly. This can help you track your progress and revisit ideas later on.
- Seek inspiration: Surround yourself with sources of inspiration, whether it's books, art, music, or nature. Exposing yourself to different stimuli can stimulate creativity.
- Practice creativity exercises: Engage in activities that stimulate your creativity, such as drawing, writing, or improvisational acting. The more you practice being creative, the easier it becomes.

Remember, creativity is a skill that can be developed with practice and perseverance. By incorporating these tips into your daily routine, you can cultivate a more creative and innovative mindset.

Discussion Questions: (Please limit to 4-5 questions that pertain to your group)

- Can you think of examples from your own life or from the world around you where creativity and innovation worked well?
- Can you identify any similarities or differences between the challenges faced by the biblical figures and challenges you encounter in your own life?
- Have you ever experienced any of these barriers to creativity and innovation personally, and how did you overcome them?
- Do you agree that creativity is a skill that can be developed with practice? Why or why not?
- Can you think of any examples from your own life where practicing creativity has led to improvement?
- How do you think embracing failure can contribute to creativity and innovation?
- Can you think of any examples from history or popular culture where failure ultimately led to success?

INFORMATION FOR INSTRUCTORS

Creativity and innovation can face various barriers, both internal and external. Here are some common Challenges:

- Fear of making mistakes: Some people are scared to try new things because they worry about failing or what others might think.
- Not feeling motivated: If you're not interested in something, it's hard to be creative about it.
- Thinking creativity is fixed: Some people believe you're either creative or you're not, which can hold them back from trying new things.
- Not having enough time: Sometimes, deadlines or schedules make it hard to spend time coming up with new ideas.
- The culture around you: If the people you work with don't value creativity or punish mistakes, it can be hard to be creative.
- Not having the right tools: Without access to things you need, like materials or money, it's tough to try out new ideas.
- Everyone thinking the same: If everyone in a group has the same ideas, it's hard to come up with something different.
- Only caring about being fast: Sometimes, people focus too much on getting things done quickly instead of coming up with new ways to do things.
- Not having different perspectives: If everyone in a group is the same, they might miss out on new ideas from different backgrounds.
- Not liking change: Some people or groups don't like doing things differently, even if it could lead to something better.

To overcome these challenges, it's important to create an environment where people feel comfortable trying new things, where everyone's ideas are valued, and where there's enough time and resources to explore creative solutions.

SUGGESTED GAME: FORTUNATELY/UNFORTUNATELY

Have all your players sit in a circle, or establish a clear playing order. Then, proceed to develop a story, with each person saying one sentence at a time. Here's the catch: each sentence must start with either "fortunately" or "unfortunately," always alternating. The story can go on and on and take different turns according to the players. Let them talk and be creative and develop the story on their own.

For example:

Player 1: I got a new puppy. Player 2: Unfortunately, it ran away. Player 3: Fortunately, it came back with a $100 bill in it's mouth! Player 3: Unfortunately, it was wet, and a corner was torn off, so I couldn't spend it. Player 4: Fortunately, the bank traded me for a new one. Player 5: Unfortunately, my mom said I had to put it into my savings account.

NOTES:

INSPIRING OTHERS
CHAPTER 39

DEFINITION

To INSPIRE OTHERS means to motivate and uplift them through your words, actions, or achievements. When you inspire someone, you ignite a sense of enthusiasm, determination, or hope within them. This could involve sharing your own successes and challenges to show what's possible, offering encouragement and support during difficult times, or simply being a positive role model. By inspiring others, you help them believe in themselves, pursue their goals, and reach their full potential. It's about making a positive impact on the lives of those around you and helping them to find their own sources of motivation and passion.

BIBLICAL REFERENCES

There are several biblical references about inspiring others. Here are a few examples:

Philippians 2:3-4 (NIV):

> *"Do nothing out of selfish ambition or vain conceit. Rather, in humility value others above yourselves, not looking to your own interests but each of you to the interests of the others."*

1 Thessalonians 5:11 (NIV):

> *"Therefore encourage one another and build each other up, just as in fact you are doing."*

Proverbs 27:17 (NIV):

> *"As iron sharpens iron, so one person sharpens another."*

Hebrews 10:24-25 (NIV):

> *"And let us consider how we may spur one another on toward love and good deeds, not giving up meeting together, as some are in the habit of doing, but encouraging one another—and all the more as you see the Day approaching."*

Matthew 5:16 (NIV):

> *"In the same way, let your light shine before others, that they may see your good deeds and glorify your Father in heaven."*

These verses emphasize the importance of humility, encouragement, mutual support, and setting a positive example for others, all of which are essential aspects of inspiring those around us according to biblical teachings.

Tips:

- Keep it simple: Use easy words and sentences that everyone can understand.
- Share stories: Tell stories that are like our own lives so we can see how people overcome problems and do great things.
- Give practical advice: Tell us what we can do right now to reach our goals or solve problems.
- Show good examples: Talk about people we look up to and what they do that's so good, like being kind or working hard.
- Think about what we want: Ask us to think about what we want to do in life and how we can get there.
- Tell us it's okay to fail: Tell us that it's normal to have problems, but we can keep trying and learn from our mistakes.
- Be supportive: Make a place where we feel safe to share our dreams and help each other.
- Celebrate success: Cheer for us when we do something good, no matter how small.
- Lead by example: Show us how to be good people by being one yourself.
- Be real: Talk to us like you're our friend, and we'll trust you more.

Discussion Questions: (Please limit to 4-5 questions that pertain to your group)

- Can you give an example of when someone made you feel excited or motivated to do something?
- Why do you think it's important to encourage and support each other?
- How does it feel when someone believes in you and cheers you on?
- Can you think of a story from the Bible where someone encouraged or helped others?
- How can we inspire others in our everyday lives?
- Can you think of something kind or helpful you could do for someone to make them feel good?
- Why is it important to celebrate the successes of others, even if they're small?
- How does it feel when someone celebrates your achievements?
- What are some qualities of a good role model?

- Can you think of someone you look up to and why they inspire you?
- How can we create a supportive environment where everyone feels safe to share their ideas and dreams?
- What can we do to help each other when we're feeling down or discouraged?
- Why is it important to be honest and genuine when trying to inspire others?
- How can being friendly and truthful help us build trust with others?
- How can showing kindness, hard work, and determination inspire others to do the same?
- Can you think of a time when someone's actions motivated you to be a better person?
- What can you do today to inspire someone around you?
- Can you think of a simple act of kindness or encouragement you can offer to make someone's day brighter?

Information for Instructors

Challenges:

- Complex language: Using vocabulary or concepts that are too advanced or unfamiliar for the audience can make it difficult for them to understand and connect with the message.
- Lack of relatability: If the content doesn't resonate with the experiences, interests, or concerns of the audience, they may struggle to see its relevance to their own lives.
- Lack of personal connection: Failing to establish a personal connection or emotional resonance with the audience can make it harder for them to engage with and be inspired by the message.
- Negative mindset or attitude: If the audience is feeling demotivated, discouraged, or cynical, they may be less receptive to being inspired and more resistant to positive messages.
- Limited accessibility: Barriers such as socioeconomic status, cultural background, or educational disparities can impact access to resources or opportunities that could facilitate inspiration.
- Overwhelming challenges: If the audience is facing significant obstacles or hardships, they may find it difficult to be inspired or motivated by messages that don't address or acknowledge their struggles.
- Lack of trust or credibility: If the speaker or source of inspiration lacks credibility or trustworthiness in the eyes of the audience, they may be less inclined to be influenced or inspired by their message.

Suggested Game: Two things

Give each member of your group a piece of paper that lists the names of all of the members of your group. Encourage everyone to write down two things that they like about each person in the group. They can also write down how the person makes them feel.

Everyone needs to hear words of affirmation and have how people feel about them confirmed. It encourages them by having proof that something about them has inspired another person.

NOTES:

PUBLIC SPEAKING
CHAPTER 40

DEFINITION

PUBLIC SPEAKING IS the act of delivering a speech or presentation to a live audience. It involves conveying information, ideas, opinions, or emotions effectively to a group of people. Public speaking can occur in various settings, including conferences, seminars, classrooms, business meetings, political rallies, and social events. Effective public speaking requires skills such as clear communication, confidence, organization, persuasion, and the ability to engage and connect with the audience. It plays a crucial role in influencing, informing, inspiring, and entertaining audiences on a wide range of topics.

BIBLICAL REFERENCES

Several biblical references touch upon the theme of public speaking and the importance of effective communication. Here are a few examples:

Proverbs 18:21 (NIV):

"The tongue has the power of life and death, and those who love it will eat its fruit."

This verse underscores the significance of words and the impact they can have on others. It emphasizes the power of speech in shaping both positive and negative outcomes.

Proverbs 15:1 (NIV):

"A gentle answer turns away wrath, but a harsh word stirs up anger."

This verse highlights the importance of choosing one's words wisely and the influence of tone and manner in communication. It suggests that speaking with kindness and humility can diffuse conflict and promote understanding.

Proverbs 25:11 (NIV):

"A word fitly spoken is like apples of gold in a setting of silver."

This verse praises the value of well-timed and appropriate speech. It suggests that eloquent and thoughtful words have a beauty and preciousness akin to fine jewelry.

Colossians 4:6 (NIV):

> *"Let your conversation be always full of grace, seasoned with salt, so that you may know how to answer everyone."*

This verse advises believers to speak graciously and with wisdom, being mindful of how they interact with others. It encourages Christians to be thoughtful and considerate in their speech, engaging with others in a respectful and persuasive manner.

These biblical references illustrate the importance of communication and public speaking in conveying messages, building relationships, and promoting understanding and harmony among people.

Tips:

Becoming a better public speaker might be tough, but it's totally doable! Here are some simple tips to help you improve:

- Practice, Practice, Practice: The more you practice speaking in front of others, the more comfortable you'll become. Start by speaking in front of a mirror or to a small group of friends or family members. You can also practice by recording yourself and watching it back to see where you can improve.

- Know Your Material: Before you speak, make sure you know your material inside and out. This will help you feel more confident and prepared. Practice your speech or presentation multiple times so you can speak about it fluently.

- Work on Your Voice and Body Language: Pay attention to how you speak and move when you're presenting. Speak clearly and loudly enough for everyone to hear you. Make eye contact with your audience and use gestures to emphasize key points. Standing up straight and smiling can also help you appear more confident.

- Slow Down: When you're nervous, it's natural to speak quickly. But speaking too fast can make it hard for your audience to understand you. Take deep breaths and try to slow down your pace. Pausing can also help you collect your thoughts and emphasize important points.

- Focus on the Audience: Remember that public speaking is about connecting with your audience. Try to engage them by asking questions, telling stories, or using examples they can relate to. Pay attention to their reactions and adjust your presentation accordingly.

- Learn from Others: Watch videos of good public speakers and pay attention to what makes them effective. Take note of their speaking style, body language, and how they engage with the audience. You can also ask for feedback from teachers, classmates, or family members to help you improve.

- Stay Positive: Finally, don't be too hard on yourself if things don't go perfectly. Public speaking takes time to master, and everyone makes mistakes. Focus on what you did well and what you can improve for next time.

By following these tips and practicing regularly, you'll become a more confident and effective public speaker in no time!

Discussion Questions: (Please limit to 4-5 questions that pertain to your group)

- How do you feel when you have to talk in front of a group? Do you feel excited, nervous, or something else?
- Why do you think people might feel nervous about speaking in public?
- Can you find any stories in the Bible where someone talked to a big group of people? How do you think their words affected the listeners?
- What are some things you can do to get ready for speaking in front of others?
- How might practicing your speech help you feel more confident?
- Why is it important to talk clearly and use your hands or face when you're speaking to a group? How can these things help keep people interested?
- How can you make your speech more fun or interesting for the people listening?
- Can you think of any ways to get an audience involved or excited about what you're saying?
- Why is it important to talk at a good speed when you're speaking in public? How might talking too fast or too slow make it hard for people to understand you?
- What are some ways you can stay calm and feel more confident when you're speaking in front of others? Can you think of any tricks to help you relax?
- Why do you think it's important to practice speaking even if it's scary at first?
- How do you think being good at public speaking could help you in the future, like in school or when you're older?
- Can you think of any jobs or situations where being a good speaker might be helpful?

INFORMATION FOR INSTRUCTORS

Challenges:

- Nervousness: Feeling scared or anxious before speaking in front of others is normal. It can make your heart race and your palms sweaty. But remember, everyone feels nervous sometimes, and with practice, it gets easier.
- Fear of Judgment: Some people worry about what others will think of them when they speak. They might be scared of making mistakes or saying something silly. But it's important to remember that everyone makes mistakes, and people are usually supportive and understanding.
- Lack of Confidence: If you don't feel confident in yourself or your abilities, it can be hard to speak up in front of others. But confidence comes with practice and believing in yourself. Start small and gradually challenge yourself to speak in front of larger groups.
- Not Knowing What to Say: Sometimes, it's hard to know where to start or what to talk about. Planning and preparing your speech in advance can help. Write down key points or practice speaking in front of a mirror or with a friend.
- Physical Symptoms: Sweating, shaking, or feeling sick to your stomach are common physical

reactions to public speaking. Taking deep breaths, practicing relaxation techniques, and focusing on your message can help calm these symptoms.

- Lack of Experience: If you haven't had much practice speaking in front of others, it can feel overwhelming. But like any skill, public speaking improves with practice. Start with small opportunities, like speaking in class or at a club meeting, and gradually work your way up to bigger audiences.

Remember, everyone faces challenges when it comes to public speaking. The key is to recognize these barriers and find ways to overcome them, whether it's through practice, preparation, or seeking support from others. With time and effort, you can become a confident and effective speaker.

SUGGESTED GAME: A STORY ABOUT ME.

Allow group members to get up one at a time and tell a story about themselves. It can be their most embarrassing moment, a comedy routine, telling the group about their favorite pet, it could be an old story or something that happened this morning. Just give each member a specific amount of time to speak to the group. While the participant is speaking, everyone else is quietly listening. Encourage the listeners to cheer and applaud once the group member concludes their story.

NOTES:

CRISIS MANAGEMENT
CHAPTER 41

DEFINITION

CRISIS MANAGEMENT IS handling a big problem or emergency. It's about staying calm and figuring out the best way to deal with tough situations like accidents, natural disasters, or serious conflicts. It involves making quick decisions, coordinating help, and trying to minimize damage or harm. Think of it as being the captain of a ship during a storm, steering it safely through rough waters to reach calmer seas.

BIBLICAL REFERENCES

The Bible contains numerous stories about leaders who navigated through various emergency situations. Here are a few examples:

Moses - Moses is a central figure in the Old Testament who led the Israelites out of slavery in Egypt. Throughout their journey in the wilderness, he faced numerous crises, including conflicts within the community, scarcity of resources like food and water, and external threats. One notable emergency was when the Israelites were trapped between the pursuing Egyptian army and the Red Sea. Moses, under divine guidance, parted the waters, allowing the Israelites to escape safely (Exodus 14).

Joseph - Joseph, the son of Jacob, faced a series of crises in his life, including being sold into slavery by his brothers and later being wrongfully imprisoned in Egypt. Despite these challenges, Joseph demonstrated strong leadership during emergencies, such as interpreting Pharaoh's dreams about an impending famine and implementing a plan to store grain during the years of abundance, which ultimately saved Egypt and surrounding regions from starvation (Genesis 41).

Nehemiah - Nehemiah served as a leader during the rebuilding of the walls of Jerusalem following the Babylonian exile. He faced opposition and threats from neighboring enemies who sought to sabotage the reconstruction efforts. Nehemiah responded with strategic planning, rallying the people to work together, and maintaining vigilance against potential attacks while simultaneously continuing the construction (Nehemiah 4).

David - Before becoming king of Israel, David encountered numerous crises and emergencies, including facing the giant Goliath when he threatened the Israelite army. David's courage, faith, and reliance on God enabled him to overcome this crisis and emerge victorious (1 Samuel 17).

Paul - The Apostle Paul experienced various emergencies during his missionary journeys, including persecution, shipwrecks, and imprisonment. Despite these challenges, Paul demonstrated resilience, faith, and effective leadership in managing these crises, often by providing encouragement to his fellow believers, maintaining hope, and trusting in God's providence (Acts 27).

These biblical examples illustrate how leaders responded to emergencies with courage, faith, wisdom, and reliance on divine guidance, providing valuable lessons for leadership during challenging times.

Tips:

Here are some tips to get better at handling crises:

- Stay Calm: When a crisis hits, try to stay calm. Take a deep breath and focus on the problem instead of panicking. Keeping a clear head will help you think more clearly and make better decisions.
- Plan Ahead: It's important to have a plan in place before a crisis happens. Think about potential emergencies that could occur and come up with a plan for how to handle them. Practice drills or simulations to prepare yourself and others.
- Communicate Effectively: Good communication is key during a crisis. Make sure to keep everyone informed about what's happening and what they need to do. Listen to others' ideas and concerns, and be open to feedback.
- Work Together: Crisis management is a team effort. Work together with others to come up with solutions and support each other during difficult times. Don't be afraid to ask for help when you need it.
- Stay Flexible: Things don't always go according to plan during a crisis, so it's important to stay flexible. Be willing to adapt your plans and strategies as the situation changes.
- Learn from Experience: After a crisis is over, take some time to reflect on what happened and what you can learn from it. Think about what went well and what could have been done better, and use that knowledge to improve your crisis management skills for next time.

By following these tips and practicing your crisis management skills, you'll be better prepared to handle emergencies when they arise.

Discussion Questions: (Please limit to 4-5 questions that pertain to your group)

- Why do you think it's important to stay calm during a crisis?
- Can you think of some examples of crises that could happen at school or home?
- How do you think planning ahead can help during a crisis?
- What are some ways good communication can be helpful during an emergency?
- How can working together as a team help during a crisis?
- Why is it important to be flexible when dealing with an emergency?

- Can you name a Bible story that involves crisis management? What happened in the story, and how was the crisis resolved?
- What can we learn from the Bible stories about crisis management?
- How can we prepare ourselves for emergencies even when they're not happening?
- Have you ever been in a situation where you needed to help during an emergency? How did you feel, and what did you do?
- Why is it important to reflect on past emergencies and learn from them?
- What are some ways we can support each other during a crisis?
- Can you think of any drills or practice exercises we could do to prepare for emergencies?
- What advice would you give to someone who is facing a crisis for the first time?

INFORMATION FOR INSTRUCTORS

Barriers to crisis management are like hurdles or obstacles that make it harder to handle emergencies effectively. Some common barriers include:

- Lack of Preparation: Not having a plan in place for emergencies can be a major barrier. Without a clear strategy or procedures to follow, it's challenging to respond quickly and efficiently when a crisis occurs.
- Poor Communication: Communication breakdowns can hinder crisis management efforts. If information isn't shared effectively or if there are misunderstandings among team members, it can delay decision-making and lead to confusion.
- Limited Resources: Inadequate resources, such as manpower, equipment, or funds, can impede crisis management. Without the necessary tools and support, it's difficult to address the needs of those affected by the emergency.
- Resistance to Change: Sometimes, people may resist implementing new strategies or adapting to changes in the crisis situation. This resistance can slow down response efforts and prevent effective crisis management.
- External Factors: External factors beyond control, such as adverse weather conditions, geopolitical tensions, or regulatory constraints, can pose significant barriers to crisis management. These factors may exacerbate the situation and make it more challenging to mitigate the crisis.

Overcoming these barriers requires proactive planning, effective communication, resource allocation, flexibility, and collaboration among all involved parties. Identifying and addressing these barriers in advance can better prepare organizations and individuals to manage crises successfully when they arise.

SUGGESTED GAME: INVITE A FIRST-RESPONDER IN YOUR COMMUNITY AS A GUEST SPEAKER

Invite a police officer, firefighter, or EMT to speak with your group. It's great to get our youth engaged with first responders and allow them to ask questions and engage. Meeting first responders before an emergency happens helps to resolve nervousness and builds trust. It could be that one of your youth members might decide to become a first responder.

NOTES:

Knowledge Sharing
Chapter 42

Definition

KNOWLEDGE SHARING MEANS giving and receiving information, ideas, and skills with others. It's like when you share your favorite book with a friend or teach someone how to play a game you know well. It's about spreading knowledge so everyone can learn and grow together.

Biblical References

Several biblical references highlight the importance of sharing knowledge and wisdom:

Proverbs 15:7 (NIV):

> *"The lips of the wise spread knowledge; not so the hearts of fools."*

This verse emphasizes that wise individuals share their knowledge willingly, contrasting them with fools who withhold it.

Proverbs 18:15 (NIV):

> *"The heart of the discerning acquires knowledge, for the ears of the wise seek it out."*

This verse emphasizes the pursuit of knowledge by those who are wise and discerning.

Proverbs 22:17-18 (NIV):

> *"Pay attention and turn your ear to the sayings of the wise; apply your heart to what I teach, for it is pleasing when you keep them in your heart and have all of them ready on your lips."*

This passage encourages listeners to actively seek and retain wisdom, indicating that sharing it with others is pleasing and beneficial.

Ecclesiastes 4:9-10 (NIV):

> *"Two are better than one, because they have a good return for their labor: If either of them falls down, one can help the other up. But pity anyone who falls and has no one to help them up."*

While not explicitly about knowledge sharing, this verse emphasizes the value of partnership and collaboration, suggesting that working together can lead to greater success and support.

These biblical passages underscore the importance of acquiring wisdom, sharing knowledge, and collaborating with others for mutual benefit and growth.

Tips:

- Use Clear Language: When explaining something, use simple and easy-to-understand words. Avoid using jargon or complicated terms that might confuse others.
- Provide Examples: Use examples or real-life situations to illustrate your points. This can help others better understand the information you're sharing.
- Be Patient: Not everyone learns at the same pace, so be patient when sharing knowledge. Take the time to answer questions and provide further explanations if needed.
- Encourage Questions: Create an open and supportive environment where people feel comfortable asking questions. This can help clarify any confusion and encourage further learning.
- Use Visual Aids: Incorporate visual aids such as diagrams, charts, or drawings to help reinforce your explanations. Visuals can make complex concepts easier to understand.
- Break it Down: If you're explaining a complex topic, break it down into smaller, more manageable parts. This makes it easier for others to grasp the information step by step.
- Use Analogies: Compare unfamiliar concepts to familiar ones using analogies. This can help bridge the gap between new information and what people already know.
- Encourage Participation: Encourage active participation by inviting others to share their thoughts and experiences. This fosters a collaborative learning environment where everyone can contribute.
- Provide Resources: Offer additional resources such as books, articles, or websites for further exploration. This allows people to delve deeper into the topic on their own time.
- Lead by Example: Be willing to share your own knowledge and experiences openly. By leading by example, you inspire others to do the same.

By following these tips, you can effectively share knowledge in a way that is accessible and engaging for everyone.

Discussion Questions: (Please limit to 4-5 questions that pertain to your group)

- Why do you think it's good to share what we know with others?
- Can you think of a time when someone helped you learn something new? How did they do it?
- How does it feel when you teach someone else something you know?

- What are some ways we can share knowledge with our friends or classmates?
- Why is it important to explain things in a way that everyone can understand?
- How can showing examples help someone understand what we're talking about?
- Have you ever had trouble understanding something? What could the person explaining it have done better?
- Why do you think it's important to encourage questions when we're teaching or sharing?
- How can pictures or drawings help when we're explaining something?
- Why do you think it's helpful to break down big ideas into smaller parts?
- What can we do to make sure everyone feels comfortable joining in and sharing their ideas?
- Where can we find more information if we want to learn more about something?
- Why is it important to show others how to share knowledge by doing it ourselves?

Information for Instructors

Barriers to knowledge sharing can be obstacles or challenges that make it difficult for people to share what they know with others. Such as:

- Lack of Trust: If someone doesn't trust others, they might not want to share their knowledge because they're worried it could be used against them or they might not get credit for it.
- Fear of Criticism: People might be afraid of being judged or criticized for what they know, so they keep their knowledge to themselves instead of sharing it openly.
- Competition: Sometimes, people feel like they're in competition with others, so they don't want to share their knowledge because they think it might give someone else an advantage over them.
- Lack of Time: People are often busy with their own tasks and responsibilities, so they might not have enough time to share what they know with others.
- Technology Challenges: If someone isn't comfortable using technology or doesn't have access to the right tools, they might find it hard to share knowledge online or through digital platforms.
- Organizational Culture: In some workplaces or communities, there might be a culture that doesn't encourage or reward knowledge sharing, which can make people hesitant to share what they know.
- Language or Communication Challenges: If someone has trouble communicating effectively or if they speak a different language than others, it can be hard for them to share their knowledge in a way that others understand.

By understanding these barriers, we can work together to find solutions and create environments where knowledge sharing is easier and more encouraged.

Suggested Game: Pictionary

You can use the board game or use a piece of paper and a pencil if you have a small group.

NOTES:

REPUTATION
CHAPTER 43

DEFINITION

REPUTATION MEANS WHAT other people think about you based on your actions and behavior. It's like your social image or how others see you. If you're known for being honest and helpful, you have a good reputation. But if you often do things that make people upset or don't keep your promises, you might have a bad reputation. Your reputation can affect how people treat you and whether they trust you. So, it's important to think about the choices you make and how they might impact what others think of you.

BIBLICAL REFERENCES

In the Bible, reputation is often referred to in terms of honor, integrity, and how one is perceived by others. Here are a few biblical references that touch on the topic:

Proverbs 22:1 (NIV):

> *"A good name is more desirable than great riches; to be esteemed is better than silver or gold."*

This verse emphasizes the value of having a good reputation, suggesting that it is more important than material wealth.

Ecclesiastes 7:1 (NIV):

> *"A good name is better than fine perfume, and the day of death better than the day of birth."*

Here, having a good name (or reputation) is compared to precious perfume, highlighting its significance.

Proverbs 27:2 (NIV):

> *"Let someone else praise you, and not your own mouth; an outsider, and not your own lips."*

This verse suggests that it is better to have others speak well of you than to boast about yourself. It implies that a good reputation is earned through the recognition and praise of others.

1 Timothy 3:7 (NIV):

> *"He must also have a good reputation with outsiders, so that he will not fall into disgrace and into the devil's trap."*

This verse specifically refers to the reputation of leaders within the Christian community, emphasizing the importance of maintaining a good reputation to avoid falling into disgrace and being ensnared by temptation.

These verses highlight the significance of reputation in the biblical context and emphasize the importance of integrity, humility, and the perception of others.

Tips:

Building a good reputation means showing others that you're trustworthy, kind, and reliable. Here are some tips on how to do that:

- Be Honest: Always tell the truth, even when it's hard. People appreciate honesty and will trust you more if they know they can rely on you to be truthful.
- Keep Your Promises: If you say you'll do something, make sure you follow through. Being dependable shows that you're someone others can count on.
- Be Kind: Treat others with respect and kindness. Small acts of kindness can go a long way in building a positive reputation.
- Be Respectful: Show respect to everyone, regardless of their background or differences. Treat others the way you want to be treated.
- Listen: Take the time to listen to others and show that you care about their thoughts and feelings. Being a good listener can help you build strong relationships.
- Be Responsible: Take responsibility for your actions and own up to your mistakes. Showing accountability demonstrates maturity and builds trust.
- Help Others: Offer to help others when you can. Whether it's lending a hand with schoolwork or volunteering in your community, being helpful shows that you're considerate and caring.
- Be Positive: Try to have a positive attitude and look for the good in every situation. Positivity is contagious and can help you build a reputation as someone who brings joy and encouragement to others.

Remember, building a good reputation takes time and consistency. By being honest, kind, and reliable, you can earn the trust and respect of those around you.

Discussion Questions: (Please limit to 4-5 questions that pertain to your group)

- How do you think our reputation affects how people see us?
- Can you think of someone you know who has a good reputation? What do they do that makes others think highly of them?
- Have you ever experienced a situation where someone's reputation affected how you treated them? How did it make you feel?
- Why do you think it's important to be honest and keep promises in building a good reputation?
- How can being kind and respectful help improve someone's reputation?
- Have you ever seen someone take responsibility for their actions, even if it meant admitting they were wrong? How did others react?
- Why do you think listening to others and showing empathy can contribute to a positive reputation?
- Can you think of a time when helping others improved someone's reputation? How did it impact the way others saw them?
- Do you agree with the Bible verses that say having a good reputation is important? Why or why not?
- What are some ways we can maintain a good reputation even when faced with challenges or temptations?
- How can having a positive attitude and spreading positivity help shape someone's reputation?
- Have you ever experienced a situation where someone's reputation was damaged because of their actions? What could they have done differently?
- What do you think it means to have integrity, and why is it important for reputation?
- Do you think reputation is more about what others think of us or how we see ourselves? Why?
- How can we encourage each other to build and maintain positive reputations in our school or community?

These questions aim to engage students in thinking critically about reputation, its importance, and how they can contribute to building positive reputations for themselves and others.

INFORMATION FOR INSTRUCTORS

Having a good reputation means being respected and trusted by others. However, there are some things that can get in the way of having a good reputation:

- Lying: If you're not honest and lie to people, they won't trust you, and your reputation can suffer.
- Breaking Promises: If you often say you'll do something but don't follow through, people might see you as unreliable, harming your reputation.
- Bullying: Being mean or hurting others can make people see you in a negative light and damage your reputation.

- Gossiping: Spreading rumors or talking behind people's backs can make others distrust you and affect your reputation.
- Cheating: Whether in school or in relationships, cheating shows dishonesty and can ruin your reputation.
- Not Keeping Secrets: If you can't be trusted to keep things confidential, people may not confide in you, harming your reputation.
- Being Selfish: Always putting yourself first without considering others can lead to a bad reputation for being uncaring or inconsiderate.

Remember, building a good reputation takes time and effort, but it's worth it because it helps you earn the trust and respect of those around you.

SUGGESTED GAME: THE COMPANY YOU KEEP

Give each team member a piece of paper and a writing utensil. Give these instructions to your youth group:

"Think of your five closest friends. Think about what you like about these friends. Your closest friends with have things in common with each other. Write down five personality traits that all five friends have in common. For example, if all five friends love to laugh, all five friends may drive nice cars, all five friends may be intelligent, or all five friends may see the world from a different point of view. Your job is to write down five personality traits that all five of your friends have in common."

After everyone has written five traits on their paper, read this:

"On your paper you thought you were writing down the traits of your friends. Looking at the list honestly, see how many of the personality traits actually describe you too. The tendency for people to associate with others who are similar to them is called homophily. Most people feel more comfortable around people who are similar to them. This feeling is also described as fitting in. That's why friendships can sometimes get in the way of building a good reputation. It may not seem fair, but people are judged by the company they keep."

NOTES:

Goal-setting
Chapter 44

Definition

GOAL SETTING IS when you decide on things you want to do and figure out how to make them happen. It's like making a plan to achieve something important. To set goals, you need to be clear about what you want to achieve, make sure you can measure your progress, make sure it's something you can realistically do, make sure it's important to you, and give yourself a deadline to finish it. Setting goals helps you stay focused and motivated to reach your dreams.

Biblical References

The Bible provides several verses and stories that offer insights into goal setting and achieving objectives. Here are a few examples:

Proverbs 16:3 (NIV):

> *"Commit to the Lord whatever you do, and he will establish your plans."*

This verse encourages individuals to entrust their plans and goals to God, emphasizing the importance of seeking divine guidance and support in achieving one's objectives.

Philippians 3:13-14 (NIV):

> *"Brothers and sisters, I do not consider myself yet to have taken hold of it. But one thing I do: Forgetting what is behind and straining toward what is ahead, I press on toward the goal to win the prize for which God has called me heavenward in Christ Jesus."*

In this passage, the apostle Paul talks about focusing on the future and working toward spiritual goals with determination and perseverance.

Proverbs 21:5 (NIV):

> *"The plans of the diligent lead to profit as surely as haste leads to poverty."*

This verse highlights the importance of careful planning and diligence in achieving success, contrasting it with the negative consequences of acting hastily or without purpose.

Luke 14:28-30 (NIV):

> *"Suppose one of you wants to build a tower. Won't you first sit down and estimate the cost to see if you have enough money to complete it? For if you lay the foundation and are not able to finish it, everyone who sees it will ridicule you, saying, 'This person began to build and wasn't able to finish.'"*

This passage illustrates the importance of counting the cost and planning carefully before embarking on a project or goal, emphasizing the need for thorough preparation and commitment.

These biblical references emphasize the significance of seeking divine guidance, staying focused on spiritual goals, working diligently, and careful planning when setting and pursuing objectives.

Tips for creating your own goals:

Goals should be S.M.A.R.T goals, which means they should be:

- Specific: Goals should be clear, well-defined, and specific, detailing exactly what is to be accomplished.
- Measurable: Goals should be quantifiable, allowing progress to be tracked and measured objectively.
- Achievable: Goals should be realistic and attainable, considering available resources, skills, and constraints.
- Relevant: Goals should align with broader objectives and be relevant to the individual or organization's mission, vision, and values.
- Time-bound: Goals should have a defined timeframe or deadline for completion, providing a sense of urgency and focus.

Breaking down large goals into smaller, manageable steps is essential for making progress and staying motivated. Here's how you can do it:

1. Identify Your Goal: First, clearly define the big goal you want to achieve. Make sure it's specific and meaningful to you.
2. Break It Into Smaller Tasks: Divide your big goal into smaller tasks or steps. These tasks should be things you can do one at a time to work towards your larger goal.
3. Set Deadlines: Assign deadlines to each of the smaller tasks. This helps you stay on track and gives you a sense of urgency.
4. Prioritize Tasks: Determine which tasks are most important or urgent. Focus on completing those first before moving on to others.
5. Create a Plan: Write down your plan for completing each task. Include details like what needs to be done, how you'll do it, and any resources you'll need.
6. Take Action: Start working on your tasks according to your plan. Take one step at a time, and don't be afraid to ask for help if you need it.

7. Track Your Progress: Keep track of your progress as you complete each task. Celebrate your accomplishments along the way to stay motivated.

8. Adjust as Needed: Be flexible and willing to adjust your plan if necessary. Sometimes, things don't go as expected, and that's okay. Learn from your experiences and keep moving forward.

Understanding the barriers to setting goals and finding ways to overcome them can help you set meaningful goals and work toward achieving them effectively. Breaking down large goals into smaller steps makes them more manageable and increases your chances of success. It also helps you stay focused and motivated throughout the process. The first step to accomplishing goals is to set them for yourself.

Discussion Questions: (Please limit to 4-5 questions that pertain to your group)

- Why do you think it's important to set goals in life?
- How can setting goals help you achieve your dreams and aspirations?
- Can you think of any personal experiences or examples where you faced the barriers to goal-setting listed?
- How do you think negative self-talk can impact our ability to set and achieve goals?
- What strategies can we use to overcome negative thoughts and beliefs about ourselves?
- In what ways can external distractions, such as social media or peer pressure, interfere with our goal-setting efforts?
- How can we minimize external distractions such as social media or peer pressure and stay focused on our objectives?
- The text mentions S.M.A.R.T. goals as a helpful framework for effective goal setting. Can you explain what each letter in S.M.A.R.T. stands for and why it's important for goals to meet these criteria?

INFORMATION FOR INSTRUCTORS

Challenges:

When it comes to setting goals, there can be things that get in the way or make it harder to achieve what you want. These are called barriers. Some common barriers to goal setting include:

- Lack of Clarity: Sometimes, you might not be clear about what you really want to achieve. If your goals are vague or unclear, it's hard to know what steps to take to reach them.
- Fear of Failure: Feeling afraid that you might not succeed can stop you from setting goals altogether or make you hesitant to pursue them. It's important to remember that making mistakes is a part of learning and growing.
- Procrastination: Putting off tasks or delaying taking action can prevent you from making progress toward your goals. Procrastination can be a barrier because it keeps you from getting started or completing important steps.
- Lack of Resources: Sometimes, you might not have the tools, time, money, or support

you need to work toward your goals. Without these resources, achieving your goals can be much harder.

- Negative Self-Talk: Negative thoughts or beliefs about yourself can hold you back from setting ambitious goals or believing in your ability to achieve them. It's important to challenge these negative thoughts and replace them with positive affirmations.
- Lack of Motivation: If you're not motivated or passionate about your goals, it can be challenging to stay committed and take consistent action. Finding ways to stay inspired and focused can help overcome this barrier.
- Distractions: External distractions, like social media, TV, or other people, can divert your attention away from your goals and make it harder to stay on track.

SUGGESTED GAME: SETTING A GROUP GOAL

Your team can set a fundraising goal or any other type of goal. The goal for our group was to double the amount of participants in one year.

NOTES:

PERSUASION
CHAPTER 45

DEFINITION

PERSUASION MEANS TRYING to convince someone to agree with you or do something you want by giving them reasons and arguments that make sense to them. It's like when you're trying to get your friends to choose pizza for dinner instead of burgers by telling them how delicious and satisfying pizza is. Persuasion is about using words and ideas to change someone's mind or influence their actions.

BIBLICAL REFERENCES

In the Bible, there are several instances where persuasion plays a significant role.

Paul's Letters: The apostle Paul often used persuasive language in his letters to the early Christian communities. For example, in his letter to the Romans, he writes, "I appeal to you, brothers and sisters, in the name of our Lord Jesus Christ, that all of you agree with one another in what you say and that there be no divisions among you, but that you be perfectly united in mind and thought" (Romans 15:5).

Jesus' Parables: Jesus frequently used parables to persuade his listeners to understand spiritual truths. One notable example is the Parable of the Good Samaritan (Luke 10:25-37), where Jesus persuades his audience to show compassion and mercy to others.

Prophetic Calls: Throughout the Old Testament, prophets like Jeremiah and Isaiah used persuasive language to call people to repentance and obedience to God's commandments. For instance, Isaiah 1:18 says, "Come now, let us reason together, says the Lord: though your sins are like scarlet, they shall be as white as snow; though they are red like crimson, they shall become like wool."

Wisdom Literature: Books like Proverbs and Ecclesiastes contain wisdom teachings that often use persuasive language to encourage readers to seek righteousness and avoid folly. Proverbs 1:10-19, for example, persuades readers to resist the temptation to join in with sinners.

These examples demonstrate how persuasion is used throughout the Bible to convey moral, spiritual, and ethical truths, urging people to make choices aligned with God's will.

Tips:

- Know your audience: Understand who you're talking to and adjust your message to match what they care about and what they know.
- Build credibility: Show that you know your stuff and can be trusted by sharing facts, examples, or your own expertise.
- Use storytelling: Capture people's attention by telling stories or sharing real-life examples that help explain your point of view.
- Highlight benefits: Focus on how your idea or argument can help others or make things better so people see why it matters to them.
- Address objections: Think about what might make someone disagree with you, and try to answer those concerns in advance to show you've thought it through.
- Use persuasive language: Choose words that are clear and convincing, avoiding overly complicated terms that might confuse people.
- Use visuals: Include pictures, charts, or videos to help illustrate your points and make them more memorable.
- Use social proof: Share stories or examples of other people who agree with you or have benefited from your ideas.
- Establish rapport: Make a connection with your audience by being understanding, respectful, and friendly.
- Call to action: Clearly explain what you want people to do next, whether it's making a decision, taking action, or continuing the conversation.

By understanding the barriers to being persuasive and following these tips can help you become more persuasive and get your message across effectively.

Discussion Questions: (Please limit to 4-5 questions that pertain to your group)

- Why is persuasion important in communication?
- Can you recall a personal experience when you encountered one of these barriers to being persuasive?
- How might understanding the cultural background and beliefs of your audience help you become more persuasive?
- Can you think of a situation where cultural differences might impact persuasive communication?
- Share an example of a time when you successfully persuaded someone to see things from your perspective.
- In what ways can storytelling be an effective tool for persuasion?
- Can you think of a story from your own life that could be used to persuade others?
- Why is it important to address objections when trying to persuade someone?
- How might anticipating and addressing objections in advance strengthen your persuasive argument?
- Can you think of a situation where a visual aid might have helped you better understand or communicate a complex idea?

INFORMATION FOR INSTRUCTORS

Challenges:

- Not being believable: If the person talking isn't seen as trustworthy or doesn't know much about the topic, it's hard to convince others.
- People not wanting to change their minds: Sometimes, people resist new ideas or different beliefs, especially if they clash with what they already think.
- Feelings getting in the way: Strong emotions like fear or doubt can stop people from being convinced by what someone else is saying.
- Only believing what fits with what you already think: People usually look for information that agrees with what they already believe. This makes it tough to get them to think differently.
- Our minds playing tricks on us: Our brains have biases that can mess with how we see things, like relying too much on information that's easy to remember or the first piece of info we hear.
- Getting overwhelmed with info: If there's too much to take in or it's too complicated, it's hard for people to understand and agree with the message.
- Not seeing why it matters: If the message doesn't seem important to the listener, they might not pay attention or care.
- Not understanding how the other person feels: Failing to see things from the other person's point of view can make it hard to get them to listen or agree with you.
- Picking the wrong time or place: Sometimes, trying to convince someone when they're busy or not in the right mood won't work.
- Language and cultural differences: If people speak different languages or come from different cultures, it can be tough to understand each other, making persuasion harder.

SUGGESTED GAME: THE PERSUASION GAME

One group member stands up and announces one of the topics below. Their job is to convince as many of the other group members as possible that their statement is correct. The person who gets the most people to agree with them wins.

Dogs are better pets than cats.

A taco is a sandwich.

Summer is better than winter.

Coke is better than Pepsi.

Pepperoni is the best pizza topping.

Fruit counts as dessert.

The number 13 is not unlucky.

People should eat to live, not live to eat.

Monday is the worst day of the week.

Clowns are more scary than funny.

Modern music is better than classical music.

Aliens live among us here on Earth.

It's OK to put ketchup on a hot dog.

Was Robin Hood a thief or a rebel hero?

It would be better to be able to fly than to be able to turn invisible.

Pluto should still be considered a planet.

It's better to be too hot than too cold.

We should allow people to go barefoot anywhere if they want to.

Fiction is better than non-fiction.

Using profanity is good for your mental health.

Leftover pizza is better cold than reheated.

It's OK to wear socks with sandals.

Being famous is actually not all that great.

GIF should be pronounced "JIFF," not "GIFF."

People shouldn't have to go to school or work on their birthdays.

NOTES:

SELF-REGULATION
CHAPTER 46

DEFINITION

SELF-REGULATION MEANS BEING able to control and manage your own actions, thoughts, and emotions. It's like being the boss of yourself, making decisions about what to do, how to behave, and how to react to different situations without always needing someone else to tell you what to do. It involves setting goals, making plans to achieve them, and being able to stay focused and disciplined to follow through with those plans, even when faced with distractions or challenges. It's like having your own internal compass to guide you in making good choices and behaving in ways that are helpful and appropriate.

BIBLICAL REFERENCES

The Bible offers several passages that touch upon the concept of self-regulation, although it might not use that exact term. Here are a few references:

Galatians 5:22-23 (NIV):

> *"But the fruit of the Spirit is love, joy, peace, forbearance, kindness, goodness, faithfulness, gentleness and self-control. Against such things there is no law."*

This verse speaks of self-control as one of the fruits of the Spirit, emphasizing its importance in living a faithful and righteous life.

Proverbs 25:28 (NIV):

> *"Like a city whose walls are broken through is a person who lacks self-control."*

This verse uses the imagery of a city without walls to illustrate the vulnerability and lack of protection that come with a lack of self-control.

1 Corinthians 9:24-27 (NIV):

> *"Do you not know that in a race all the runners run, but only one gets the prize? Run in such a way as to get the prize. Everyone who competes in the games goes into strict training. They do it to get a crown that will not last, but we do it to get a crown that will last forever. Therefore I do not run like someone running aimlessly; I do not fight like a boxer beating the air. No, I strike a blow to my body and make it my slave so that after I have preached to others, I myself will not be disqualified for the prize."*

This passage compares the discipline and self-control required in athletic training to the spiritual discipline needed for a Christian life.

Titus 2:11-12 (NIV):

> *"For the grace of God has appeared that offers salvation to all people. It teaches us to say 'No' to ungodliness and worldly passions, and to live self-controlled, upright and godly lives in this present age."*

Here, self-control is mentioned as part of the transformation that comes from receiving God's grace, guiding believers to live in a manner consistent with their faith.

These passages, among others, highlight the importance of self-control and disciplined living in the context of Christian faith and moral conduct.

Tips:

- Identify Triggers: Triggers are situations or emotions that often lead you to lose control. Knowing your triggers can help you prepare to manage them better.
- Practice Mindfulness: Mindfulness techniques, like deep breathing or meditation, can help you stay calm and focused in challenging situations.
- Set Clear Goals: Define what you want to achieve and break it down into smaller, manageable steps. Having clear goals can keep you motivated and on track.
- Create Routines: Establishing daily routines can help you build habits and reduce the need for constant decision-making, making it easier to stay on course.
- Use Visualization: Picture yourself successfully managing a difficult situation or reaching your goals. Visualizing success can boost your confidence and motivation.
- Take Breaks: When you're feeling overwhelmed or stressed, take a break to recharge. Stepping away from a situation temporarily can help you come back with a clearer mind.
- Develop Coping Strategies: Find healthy ways to cope with stress or negative emotions, such as talking to a friend, exercising, or practicing a hobby.
- Practice Self-Compassion: Be kind to yourself when you make mistakes or face setbacks. Treat yourself with the same kindness and understanding you would offer to a friend.
- Seek Support: Don't be afraid to reach out to friends, family, or a therapist for support and guidance when you're struggling.

- Celebrate Progress: Acknowledge and celebrate your successes, no matter how small. Recognizing your achievements can boost your confidence and motivation to keep going.

Remember, improving self-regulation takes time and practice, so be patient with yourself as you work on developing these skills.

Discussion Questions: (Please limit to 4-5 questions that pertain to your group)

- Can you think of examples from your own life where you've had to use self-regulation?
- How might recognizing the barriers help you overcome them?
- Which of the tips for self-regulation do you find most helpful or relevant to your own life?
- Reflecting on your own experiences, what are some situations where you've struggled with self-regulation?
- How do you feel about the idea of being in control of your own actions, thoughts, and emotions?
- Who are some people or resources you could turn to for support in improving your self-regulation skills?
- How might seeking support from others make it easier to work on self-regulation?
- The tips reference triggers that may cause you to lose self-regulation. Do you have triggers you could share?

INFORMATION FOR INSTRUCTORS

Barriers to self-regulation are things that can make it hard for you to control your actions, thoughts, and feelings. Here are some common ones:

- Not Knowing Yourself: If you don't understand your emotions or what makes you react in certain ways, it's tough to control yourself.
- Stress: When you're really stressed out, it's harder to make good choices and stay calm.
- Strong Feelings: Big emotions like anger or sadness can take over and make it tough to think clearly or act calmly.
- Feeling Tired: When you're exhausted, it's harder to control yourself and resist doing things you shouldn't.
- Things Around You: Distractions or a messy environment can make it tough to focus and keep yourself in check.
- Peer Pressure: Feeling pressure from friends or others can make it hard to stick to your own plans or values.
- Habits: Things you do without thinking, whether good or bad, can be hard to change even when you want to.
- Not Believing in Yourself: If you doubt your ability to control yourself, it's harder to make positive changes.
- Acting Quickly: Sometimes, doing things without thinking can lead to trouble because you didn't take the time to consider the consequences.

- Trouble Thinking Clearly: If you have difficulty paying attention, remembering things, or planning, it can be tough to control your behavior.

Working on understanding yourself better, finding ways to relax when stressed, and surrounding yourself with supportive people and environments can help you overcome these barriers and improve your self-control.

SUGGESTED GAME: FREEZE DANCE

The first thing you should know is that most teens have music on their phones. The second thing you should know is that they will not want to dance because they might feel they'll embarrass themselves. So, make it silly. Choose an older dance like the twist, macarena, or the robot and play freeze dance. Have the person playing the music to stop the music. When the music stops, the one that doesn't stop moving has to drop out. The last person still dancing wins.

NOTES:

Emotional Influence
Chapter 47

Definition

EMOTIONAL INFLUENCE MEANS that our feelings or emotions can affect the way we think, act, or make decisions. It's like when something makes us happy, sad, excited, or scared, it can change how we see things or what choices we make. For example, if a sad movie makes us cry, it's because the story has emotionally influenced us. Emotions can have a big impact on how we understand stories, relate to others, and even learn new things.

Biblical References:

In the Bible, there are numerous references to emotions and their influence on human behavior, relationships, and decisions. Here are a few examples:

Proverbs 15:13:

"A glad heart makes a cheerful face, but by sorrow of heart the spirit is crushed."

This verse suggests that emotions like joy or sorrow can have a visible impact on a person's outward demeanor and inner state.

Ephesians 4:26-27:

"In your anger do not sin: Do not let the sun go down while you are still angry, and do not give the devil a foothold."

This passage acknowledges the presence of emotions like anger but advises against letting them control actions or linger unresolved, as they can lead to negative consequences.

Proverbs 14:30:

"A heart at peace gives life to the body, but envy rots the bones."

Here, emotions such as peace and envy are contrasted, highlighting how they can affect not only mental well-being but also physical health.

James 1:19-20:

> *"My dear brothers and sisters, take note of this: Everyone should be quick to listen, slow to speak and slow to become angry because human anger does not produce the righteousness that God desires."*

This verse emphasizes the importance of managing emotions like anger through patience and restraint, suggesting that unchecked emotions can hinder spiritual growth.

Psalm 51:10:

> *"Create in me a pure heart, O God, and renew a steadfast spirit within me."*

This prayer of King David reflects a desire for emotional renewal and purification, acknowledging the need for divine intervention to overcome negative emotions and cultivate positive ones.

These biblical references demonstrate the recognition of emotions as powerful forces that can influence thoughts, actions, and spiritual well-being, and they offer guidance on how to navigate and manage them in accordance with spiritual principles.

Tips:

Using emotional influence means using feelings to persuade or affect others in a positive way. Here are some tips to help you do that:

- Understand Your Emotions: Pay attention to how you're feeling and why. When you understand your own emotions, you can better understand how they might influence others.
- Empathize with Others: Put yourself in someone else's shoes and try to understand how they might be feeling. Showing empathy can help you connect with them emotionally.
- Use Stories and Examples: Share stories or examples that evoke emotions related to your message. People often remember stories better than facts and statistics, and they can be more emotionally impactful.
- Be Authentic: People are more likely to be influenced by someone who is genuine and sincere. Be honest about your own emotions and experiences.
- Listen Actively: Pay attention to how others are feeling by actively listening to them. Acknowledge their emotions and respond empathetically.
- Appeal to Values: Connect your message to values that resonate emotionally with your audience. When people feel like something aligns with their values, they're more likely to be influenced by it.
- Use Positive Reinforcement: Offer praise or rewards when people respond positively to your message. Positive reinforcement can strengthen the emotional connection and encourage desired behavior.
- Create a Positive Environment: Surround yourself with positivity and create an atmosphere where people feel comfortable expressing their emotions.

By using these tips, you can harness the power of emotional influence to effectively communicate your message and connect with others on a deeper level.

Discussion Questions: (Please limit to 4-5 questions that pertain to your group)

- Have you ever felt happy or sad about something, and then it made you do something differently? Can you think of an example?
- The Bible talks about how emotions can affect us. Do you think it's similar to how you feel sometimes? Can you share a story from the Bible that you think shows this?
- How do you think emotions can help us understand each other better?
- Can you think of a time when understanding someone's feelings helped you get along better with them?
- Which tip for using emotional influence do you think is the easiest to do? Why?
- Do you think people in different countries feel emotions the same way, or do you think it might be different? Why?
- Sometimes people try to make us feel a certain way on purpose. How can we tell if they're trying to be helpful or if they're trying to trick us?
- How do you think being able to understand and control our emotions can help us make good choices?
- Do you think praying or having faith can help us feel better when we're having strong emotions? Why or why not?
- Can you think of a time when someone tried to make you feel a certain way, but you didn't like it? What did you do?
- How can we make sure we're using our feelings to help ourselves and others, instead of using them to hurt or control others?

INFORMATION FOR INSTRUCTORS

Challenges:

Barriers to having emotional influence are things that can get in the way of our emotions affecting us or others. Here are some barriers explained in simpler terms:

- Emotional Suppression: Sometimes we try to ignore or hide our feelings because we think they're not okay to express. This can stop our emotions from having an impact on us or others.
- Lack of Awareness: If we're not aware of our own emotions or the emotions of others, it's hard for those feelings to influence our thoughts or actions.
- Negative Environment: Being in a negative or stressful environment can make it difficult for positive emotions to shine through and influence us.
- Emotional Overload: When we're dealing with too many emotions at once, it can be overwhelming and make it hard for any single emotion to have a clear influence on us.
- Emotional Blockage: Sometimes, past experiences or trauma can create barriers that block the flow of emotions, making it hard for them to influence us in healthy ways.
- Lack of Empathy: If we're not able to understand or empathize with the emotions of others, it's harder for their feelings to influence our behavior or our relationship with them.

By recognizing these barriers, we can work to overcome them and allow emotions to have a positive influence on ourselves and those around us.

SUGGESTED GAME: THE SHARE CIRCLE WITH A VARIABLE.

With participants in a circle, ask them to complete the sentences listed. Participants can answer some or all of the questions. If you have a small group, you can ask each group member to answer the questions. If you have a larger group, go around the circle one at a time and ask individuals different questions.

The variable in this version of the game is to really think about the true emotion each person is feeling. Some participants may say they feel angry about something when they're really feeling hurt or afraid. Have them take time to truly delve into what they are really feeling.

I feel angry when…

I feel joyful when…

I feel unhappy when…

I feel hope when…

I wish I didn't have to…

I enjoy…

I feel afraid when…

Something I'd like to change is…

If I were (name a person), I would…

I feel like no one loves me when…

I know I am loved when…

Something I find boring is…

I know I can trust…

I admire (name a person) because…

I feel serene when…

I am most interested in….

I am annoyed when…

I disapprove of…

I am optimistic when

NOTES:

Courageous Vulnerability
Chapter 48

Definition

Courageous vulnerability means having the bravery to show your true self, even if it means being open about your fears, mistakes, or uncertainties. It's about being honest and real with others, even when it feels scary or uncomfortable. Instead of pretending to be perfect, a leader who shows courageous vulnerability isn't afraid to admit when they don't have all the answers or when they've made a mistake. This openness helps build trust and connection within a team because it shows that it's okay to be human and that everyone can learn and grow together.

Biblical References

In the Bible, there are several instances where individuals exhibit courageous vulnerability, although the term itself may not be explicitly used. Here are a few examples:

David and Goliath (1 Samuel 17): David, a young shepherd boy, demonstrates courageous vulnerability when he volunteers to face the giant Goliath in battle. Despite being smaller and less experienced than his opponent, David trusts in God and confronts Goliath with bravery and faith.

Peter's Denial (Matthew 26:69-75): Peter, one of Jesus' disciples, exhibits courageous vulnerability when he denies knowing Jesus three times out of fear for his own safety. Despite his initial denial, Peter later shows vulnerability by openly repenting and seeking forgiveness for his actions.

Jesus' Agony in the Garden (Matthew 26:36-46): Jesus demonstrates courageous vulnerability in the Garden of Gethsemane when he prays to God, expressing his anguish and fear about the impending crucifixion. He asks God if there is any other way, yet ultimately submits to God's will with unwavering trust and obedience.

Paul's Thorn in the Flesh (2 Corinthians 12:7-10): The apostle Paul shows courageous vulnerability when he speaks about his "thorn in the flesh," a source of suffering or weakness. Despite his vulnerability, Paul finds strength in God's grace, recognizing that God's power is made perfect in weakness.

These biblical examples illustrate the concept of courageous vulnerability through acts of honesty, humility, and reliance on God's strength in the face of challenges and uncertainties.

Becoming courageously vulnerable can be challenging, but it's an important skill that can help you build deeper connections with others and grow as a person. Here are some tips to help you become more courageously vulnerable:

- Recognize Your Feelings: Start by acknowledging your emotions and understanding that it's okay to feel vulnerable sometimes. Whether you're feeling scared, sad, or unsure, allow yourself to experience and express your feelings without judgment.
- Share Your Thoughts and Feelings: Practice opening up to trusted friends, family members, or mentors about your thoughts, fears, and struggles. Sharing your experiences with others can help you feel less alone and strengthen your relationships.
- Take Small Steps: You don't have to dive into deep conversations all at once. Start by sharing small bits of yourself gradually, and as you become more comfortable, you can gradually increase your level of vulnerability.
- Be Honest with Yourself: Be honest with yourself about your strengths, weaknesses, and areas where you need help or support. Accepting yourself fully, which includes your flaws, can help you feel more confident in sharing your true self with others.
- Set Boundaries: While it's important to be open and honest, it's also important to set boundaries and protect your emotional well-being. Only share what feels comfortable and safe for you, and don't feel pressured to disclose more than you're ready for.
- Practice Self-Compassion: Be kind to yourself and practice self-compassion as you navigate vulnerability. Remember that everyone has moments of vulnerability, and it's a natural part of being human.
- Seek Support: Surround yourself with supportive people who accept you for who you are and encourage you to be yourself. Having a strong support network can give you the courage to be more vulnerable and authentic in your relationships.

By practicing these tips and being patient with yourself, you can gradually become more courageously vulnerable and experience the benefits of deeper connections and personal growth.

Discussion Questions: (Please limit to 4-5 questions that pertain to your group)

- Can you think of any personal experiences where you or someone else demonstrated courageous vulnerability?
- How do you think showing your true self, even when it's scary or uncomfortable, can impact your relationships with others?
- In what ways do you think courageous vulnerability can help build trust and connection within a team or community?
- How can societal norms and cultural expectations influence our willingness to show vulnerability?
- How do you think self-compassion plays a role in becoming more courageously vulnerable?
- Can you think of any ways to practice self-compassion in your own life?

INFORMATION FOR INSTRUCTORS

Courageous vulnerability can be challenging due to various barriers that individuals may encounter. Here are some common Challenges:

- Fear of Rejection: People may fear that if they show vulnerability, others will reject or criticize them. This fear can stem from past experiences of rejection or a desire to maintain a certain image or reputation.

- Social Stigma: Society often associates vulnerability with weakness, which can discourage individuals from being open about their feelings, struggles, or imperfections. This stigma may lead people to believe that they need to appear strong and self-sufficient at all times.

- Cultural Norms: Cultural norms and expectations can influence how individuals express vulnerability. In some cultures, there may be pressure to maintain a stoic demeanor and avoid showing emotions or admitting weaknesses.

- Trust Issues: Building trust is essential for being vulnerable, but past betrayals or breaches of trust can make it difficult for individuals to open up to others. Without trust, people may hesitate to share their true thoughts and feelings for fear of being hurt or betrayed again.

- Self-Doubt: Individuals may struggle with feelings of inadequacy or self-doubt, questioning whether they are worthy of love, acceptance, or support. This self-doubt can prevent them from being vulnerable with others, as they may fear being judged or rejected for who they truly are.

- Lack of Role Models: Without positive examples of courageous vulnerability, individuals may not know how to express their feelings or share their struggles openly. The absence of role models who demonstrate healthy vulnerability can make it harder for people to develop this trait themselves.

Overcoming these barriers requires self-awareness, courage, and a willingness to challenge societal norms and personal fears. Building trusting relationships, practicing self-compassion, and seeking support from others can also help individuals develop the confidence to be courageously vulnerable.

SUGGESTED GAME: CHARADES

Begin with a bowl of phrases and/or titles. In turn, each player draws a slip from the bowl and acts out the phrase shown using hand signals and body motions but no spoken words. Players then try to guess the title/phrase.

Insider tip:

There are many online tools for choosing charade words, phrases, or titles.

Do not allow teens to choose their own words and phrases to act out; even church youth groups can sometimes behave inappropriately.

Notes:

EMPATHETIC COMMUNICATION
CHAPTER 49

DEFINITION

EMPATHETIC COMMUNICATION IS when you talk to someone in a way that shows you understand and care about their feelings. It's like putting yourself in their shoes to really get how they're feeling. Instead of just saying what you think, you listen carefully to what they're saying and respond in a way that shows you're thinking about how they feel. It's all about showing kindness, understanding, and support in your words and actions.

BIBLICAL REFERENCES

Empathetic communication, though not explicitly mentioned in those terms, can be found throughout the Bible in various teachings and examples of compassion, understanding, and empathy. Here are a few biblical references that exemplify empathetic communication:

Romans 12:15 (NIV):

> *"Rejoice with those who rejoice; mourn with those who mourn."*

This verse encourages empathy by instructing believers to share in both the joys and sorrows of others, demonstrating understanding and compassion.

Philippians 2:4 (NIV):

> *"Not looking to your own interests but each of you to the interests of the others."*

This verse emphasizes the importance of considering the feelings and needs of others, which is fundamental to empathetic communication.

Colossians 3:12-13 (NIV):

> *"Therefore, as God's chosen people, holy and dearly loved, clothe yourselves with compassion, kindness, humility, gentleness and patience. Bear with each other and forgive one another if any of you has a grievance against someone. Forgive as the Lord forgave you."*

These verses highlight the virtues of compassion, kindness, and forgiveness, all of which are essential components of empathetic communication.

Proverbs 25:11 (NIV):

> *"A word fitly spoken is like apples of gold in a setting of silver."*

This verse emphasizes the importance of choosing words carefully and speaking with sensitivity, which is integral to effective, empathetic communication.

James 1:19 (NIV):

> *"My dear brothers and sisters, take note of this: Everyone should be quick to listen, slow to speak and slow to become angry."*

This verse underscores the value of active listening, patience, and restraint in communication, all of which are crucial elements of empathy.

While these verses may not explicitly use the term "empathetic communication," they provide valuable insights and guidance on how to communicate with empathy, understanding, and compassion, reflecting principles that are consistent with empathetic communication.

Tips:

- Listen Carefully: Pay close attention to what the other person is saying. Look them in the eye and try to understand their words and feelings.
- Show Understanding: Let the person know that you understand how they feel. You can say things like, "That sounds really tough," or "I can see why you feel that way."
- Use Open Body Language: Face the person, nod your head, and use gestures to show that you're interested and engaged in what they're saying.
- Ask Questions: Don't be afraid to ask questions to clarify what the person is feeling or experiencing. This shows that you care about understanding them better.
- Validate Their Feelings: Let the person know that it's okay to feel the way they do. You can say things like, "It's completely normal to feel that way," or "I would feel the same if I were in your shoes."
- Avoid Judging: Try not to judge or criticize the person for how they feel. Everyone's experiences and emotions are valid, even if they're different from yours.
- Share Your Own Feelings: If appropriate, you can share similar experiences or feelings to show that you understand what the person is going through.

- Be Patient and Supportive: Empathetic communication takes time and patience. Be there for the person and offer your support as they express themselves.
- Follow Up: Check in with the person later to see how they're doing. This shows that you care about their well-being beyond just the current conversation.

By following these tips, you can communicate more empathetically and build stronger connections with others.

Discussion Questions: (Please limit to 4-5 questions that pertain to your group)

- Why is it so important to listen carefully when we're talking to someone and trying to understand their feelings?
- What are some things that might make it hard for us to really understand how someone else is feeling when we talk to them?
- Can you think of a time when you assumed you knew how someone felt without really asking them? How might this affect our conversations?
- How can being empathetic and understanding help us make better connections with the people around us?
- Sometimes, we might feel scared to share our own feelings with others. Why do you think this is, and how can we get past this fear?
- Think about a time when someone really understood and cared about how you felt. How did it make you feel, and what did they do to show that they cared?
- What are some simple things we can do to show empathy and understanding in our everyday conversations?

INFORMATION FOR INSTRUCTORS

Barriers to empathetic communication are things that can get in the way of truly understanding and connecting with others' feelings. Here are some:

- Prejudice: This means having unfair or negative opinions about someone before you really know them. It can stop you from seeing things from their perspective.
- Assumptions: Assuming means thinking you know how someone feels or what they need without really asking or listening to them. It can lead to misunderstandings and hurt feelings.
- Lack of Listening: Sometimes, we're so focused on what we want to say next that we don't really hear what the other person is saying. This can make them feel ignored or unimportant.
- Judgment: When we judge others, we're not really trying to understand them. Instead, we're putting them down or criticizing them, which can make them feel defensive and closed off.
- Emotional Baggage: This means bringing your own past experiences and feelings into a conversation, which can cloud your understanding of what the other person is going through.
- Fear of Vulnerability: Being empathetic means being open and vulnerable to others'

emotions. Some people are scared to do this because they're afraid of getting hurt or feeling too much.

These barriers can make it harder to connect with others and show them that we care. But by being aware of them, we can work to overcome them and communicate more empathetically.

SUGGESTED GAME: BROKEN TELEPHONE

The broken telephone game is played by having a group of people sit in a circle. One person chooses a phrase or message to whisper into the ear of the person next to them. The next person then whispers the message to the next person in the circle. The game continues until the last person has heard the phrase. At the end, the last person states the phrase out loud to see how close it is to the original message. The game encourages listening skills.

NOTES:

ASSERTIVENESS
CHAPTER 50

DEFINITION

ASSERTIVENESS MEANS STANDING up for yourself in a confident way without being mean or aggressive. It's about expressing your thoughts, feelings, and needs clearly and respectfully. Being assertive means speaking up for what you believe in and setting boundaries to protect yourself while also considering the feelings of others.

BIBLICAL REFERENCES

Ephesians 6:10-18: This passage talks about putting on the armor of God to stand firm against spiritual battles. It encourages believers to be strong and assertive in their faith.

Proverbs 31:8-9: This verse instructs individuals to speak up for those who cannot speak for themselves, asserting justice and defending the rights of the poor and needy.

Matthew 5:37: In the Sermon on the Mount, Jesus teaches about the importance of integrity in speech, saying, "Let your 'Yes' be 'Yes,' and your 'No,' 'No.'" This can be interpreted as encouraging assertiveness in communication being clear and truthful.

1 Peter 3:15: This verse encourages believers to always be prepared to give an answer to anyone who asks about their faith but to do so with gentleness and respect. It suggests assertively sharing one's beliefs while also being considerate of others.

Joshua 1:9: Joshua is encouraged to be strong and courageous in leading the Israelites into the promised land, which can be seen as a call to assertiveness in fulfilling God's purposes.

These verses highlight the importance of being assertive in standing up for one's beliefs, defending what is right, and expressing oneself honestly and respectfully.

Tips:

- Practice Speaking Up: Start by expressing your thoughts and feelings in small situations, like with friends or family. This can help build your confidence in speaking your mind.
- Use "I" Statements: Instead of blaming others or making accusations, use "I" statements to

express how you feel. For example, say, "I feel hurt when..." instead of "You always make me feel bad."

- Set Boundaries: Figure out what you're comfortable with and what you're not, and then communicate those limits clearly to others. For example, say, "I need some alone time right now" if you need space.
- Practice Active Listening: When someone else is speaking, really listen to what they're saying without interrupting. This shows respect and can help build better communication.
- Be Confident: Stand tall, make eye contact, and speak in a clear, steady voice. Even if you feel nervous inside, acting confident on the outside can help you feel more assertive.
- Practice Problem-Solving: If there's a conflict or disagreement, focus on finding a solution together rather than arguing or blaming each other.
- Accept Feedback: Be open to hearing what others have to say, even if it's criticism. Use feedback as an opportunity to learn and grow.
- Practice Assertiveness Exercises: Role-play different scenarios with a friend or family member to practice assertive communication in a safe environment.

Remember, becoming more assertive takes time and practice, so be patient with yourself as you work on these skills.

Discussion Questions: (Please limit to 4-5 questions that pertain to your group)

- How do you think being assertive differs from being aggressive or passive?
- In what ways do you think being assertive can benefit your relationships with friends, family, and classmates?
- How do you think cultural or social norms can influence someone's ability to be assertive?
- Can you think of a time when you wished you had been more assertive?
- Why is active listening an important aspect of assertive communication?
- How might practicing assertiveness in small situations help you become more confident in speaking your mind in larger or more challenging situations?
- How can feedback help you improve your assertiveness skills?

INFORMATION FOR INSTRUCTORS

Barriers to being assertive are obstacles that can make it hard for someone to speak up for themselves or express their needs and feelings confidently. Here are some examples:

- Fear of Rejection: This means worrying that others might not like or accept you if you assert yourself, so you stay quiet to avoid being rejected.
- Low Self-Esteem: Feeling like you're not as good as others can hold you back from speaking up because you might doubt your worth or think your opinions don't matter.
- Conflict Avoidance: Some people don't like disagreements or arguments, so they avoid speaking up to keep the peace, even if it means not expressing their true feelings.
- People-Pleasing: Wanting to make others happy all the time can make it hard to be assertive because you might prioritize their needs over your own, even when it's not good for you.

- Lack of Communication Skills: Not knowing how to express yourself clearly or feeling unsure about what to say can be a barrier to being assertive.
- Cultural or Social Norms: Sometimes, cultural or social expectations can discourage assertiveness, especially if there's a belief that being quiet and obedient is better than speaking up.

These barriers can make it challenging for someone to assert themselves, but learning to overcome them can help build confidence and improve communication skills.

SUGGESTED GAME: FAMOUS PAIRS

Needed: Post-it notes

1. Make a list of famous pairs like Batman and Robin, Mario and Luigi, Mickey and Minnie Mouse, Romeo and Juliet, Peanut Butter and Jelly, or hands and gloves.
2. Give each person a sticky note with one-half of a famous pair written on it. For example, one person might get "Batman," and another might get "Robin."
3. Everyone walks around the room and asks each person up to three yes-or-no questions to figure out who they are. For example, they might ask, "Am I a superhero?" or "Do I wear a cape?"
4. Once someone figures out who they are, they need to find their partner. But they can't reveal who they are until their partner has also figured it out.

Have fun trying to figure out your famous pair!

NOTES:

PERSPECTIVE-TAKING
CHAPTER 51

DEFINITION

PERSPECTIVE-TAKING IS THE ability to understand how someone else feels, thinks, or sees things. It's like putting yourself in someone else's shoes to understand their point of view. Instead of just thinking about your own thoughts and feelings, perspective-taking helps you imagine what someone else might be thinking or feeling in a situation. It's an important skill for understanding others and showing empathy.

BIBLICAL REFERENCES

The Bible contains several passages that emphasize the importance of perspective-taking, compassion, and understanding others. Here are a few examples:

Philippians 2:3-4 (NIV):

> *"Do nothing out of selfish ambition or vain conceit. Rather, in humility, value others above yourselves, not looking to your own interests but each of you to the interests of the others."*

Matthew 7:12 (NIV):

> *"So in everything, do to others what you would have them do to you, for this sums up the Law and the Prophets."*

Romans 12:15 (NIV):

> *"Rejoice with those who rejoice; mourn with those who mourn."*

Galatians 6:2 (NIV):

> *"Carry each other's burdens, and in this way you will fulfill the law of Christ."*

Luke 6:31 (NIV):

> *"Do to others as you would have them do to you."*

These verses highlight the importance of considering others' perspectives, treating them with empathy, and acting with kindness and understanding towards them, which are all fundamental aspects of perspective-taking.

Tips:

Growing perspective-taking skills means becoming better at understanding how others feel, think, and see the world. Here are some tips to help you improve your perspective-taking abilities:

- Listen actively: Pay attention when others talk. Try to understand their feelings and thoughts by listening carefully to what they say. Avoid interrupting and really focus on what they're saying.
- Put yourself in their shoes: Imagine what it would be like to be in the other person's situation. Think about how you would feel and what you would think if you were them. This can help you understand their perspective better.
- Ask questions: Don't be afraid to ask questions to clarify or learn more about someone else's point of view. Asking questions shows that you're interested in understanding them better.
- Practice empathy: Empathy is the ability to understand and share the feelings of others. Try to imagine how someone else might be feeling in a particular situation. Show empathy by acknowledging their emotions and offering support.
- Consider different viewpoints: Recognize that people may have opinions, beliefs, and experiences different from yours. Be open to considering different perspectives and try to see things from their point of view, even if you disagree with them.
- Learn about different cultures and backgrounds: Take the time to learn about different cultures, backgrounds, and experiences. Learning about other cultures can help you understand and appreciate the diversity of perspectives in the world.
- Practice kindness and compassion: Treat others with kindness and compassion. Show empathy and understanding towards others, even if you don't always agree with them.
- Reflect: Reflect on your own beliefs and biases. Be aware of any prejudices and work to challenge and overcome them.

By practicing these tips, you can develop your perspective-taking skills and become better at understanding and empathizing with others.

Discussion Questions: (Please limit to 4-5 questions that pertain to your group)

- How would you explain perspective-taking to someone who doesn't understand?
- Why is it important to consider other people's feelings and thoughts?
- Can you think of a time when someone considered your feelings, and how did it make you feel?
- Which of the tips for growing perspective-taking skills do you find most helpful or interesting?

- Can you think of a situation where understanding someone else's perspective could have helped resolve a conflict or misunderstanding?
- How can we encourage others to develop their perspective-taking skills?
- Why do you think it's important to recognize and challenge our own biases?
- In what ways do you think perspective-taking skills can benefit relationships, both personally and socially?

Information for Instructors

Barriers to perspective-taking are things that can make it difficult for someone to understand or see things from another person's point of view. Here are some common barriers to perspective-taking:

- Self-centeredness: Sometimes, people are so focused on themselves and their own feelings that they find it hard to think about how others might feel.
- Lack of empathy: Empathy means understanding and sharing the feelings of others. If someone lacks empathy, they might struggle to imagine what someone else is going through.
- Misunderstandings: People might have different backgrounds, experiences, or beliefs that make it hard for them to see things the same way. This can lead to misunderstandings and make it challenging to take someone else's perspective.
- Prejudice: Prejudice is when someone has unfair feelings or opinions about a group of people based on things like their race, religion, or appearance. Prejudice can prevent someone from seeing things from another person's point of view because they're too focused on stereotypes or biases.
- Communication Challenges: Sometimes, language or communication differences can get in the way of understanding others. If someone doesn't speak the same language or has trouble expressing themselves, it can be hard to connect and see things from their perspective.
- Lack of experience: People might not have experienced certain situations themselves, so it can be hard for them to understand how someone else feels in that situation.

By recognizing these barriers, we can work to overcome them and become better at understanding and empathizing with others.

Suggested Game: Three-legged Race.

1. Divide players into pairs.
2. Have them stand shoulder-to-shoulder with their partner.
3. Tie the inside legs of each partner together with a scarf, rope, rubberband, or string.
4. Mark off a starting and ending line.
5. Race to the finish line as a team.
6. The first team to reach the finish line wins.

In a three-legged race, the left foot of one runner is strapped to the right foot of the other runner. The goal is to work together as a team to beat the other pairs to the finish line.

*Please make sure you have a safe area to play the game. You can also research other games for perspective-taking skills.

Notes:

SOCIAL ETIQUETTE
CHAPTER 52

DEFINITION

SOCIAL SKILLS ARE like tools that help you get along with others. They're how you communicate, make friends, and work well in groups. Good social skills mean being friendly, listening to others, and understanding how your actions affect people around you. It's like having a map to navigate social situations smoothly.

BIBLICAL REFERENCES

Several biblical references provide guidance on social skills and interactions such as:

Proverbs 18:24:

> *"A man of many companions may come to ruin, but there is a friend who sticks closer than a brother."*

This verse emphasizes the value of genuine friendships over superficial relationships.

Proverbs 15:1:

> *"A gentle answer turns away wrath, but a harsh word stirs up anger."*

This verse teaches the importance of speaking kindly and diplomatically in social situations to prevent conflict.

Proverbs 17:17:

> *"A friend loves at all times, and a brother is born for a time of adversity."*

Here, the enduring loyalty and support of true friendship are highlighted.

Proverbs 27:17:

> *"As iron sharpens iron, so one person sharpens another."*

This verse illustrates the concept of mutual growth and improvement through positive social interactions.

1 Thessalonians 5:11:

> *"Therefore encourage one another and build each other up, just as in fact you are doing."*

This verse underscores the importance of supporting and uplifting others through words and actions.

Matthew 7:12:

> *"So in everything, do to others what you would have them do to you, for this sums up the Law and the Prophets."*

Known as the Golden Rule, this verse teaches empathy and consideration for others in all social interactions.

These biblical references provide valuable insights into how individuals should conduct themselves in social settings, emphasizing qualities such as kindness, loyalty, empathy, and mutual support.

Tips for social etiquette:

- Practice Listening: Pay attention when others are talking. Show you're interested by nodding and asking questions about what they're saying.
- Smile and Make Eye Contact: Smiling and looking people in the eye shows that you're friendly and approachable.
- Start Conversations: Don't be afraid to say hello or ask someone how their day is going. Simple questions can lead to interesting conversations.
- Find Common Interests: Look for things you have in common with others, like hobbies or favorite movies. This can help you bond and connect more easily.
- Be Kind and Respectful: Treat others the way you want to be treated. Be polite, say please and thank you, and avoid being mean or rude.
- Practice Empathy: Try to understand how others might be feeling. Put yourself in their shoes and show that you care about their emotions.
- Join Clubs or Activities: Getting involved in clubs, sports teams, or other group activities can give you more opportunities to meet new people and practice your social skills.
- Don't Be Afraid to Make Mistakes: Everyone messes up sometimes. Don't let fear of embarrassment hold you back from trying to make friends or participate in social activities.
- Ask for Help When You Need It: If you're struggling with social skills, don't be afraid to ask a trusted adult, like a teacher or parent, for advice or support.
- Practice, Practice, Practice: Like any skill, social skills get better with practice. Keep trying, and don't get discouraged if things don't go perfectly the first time.

Remember, building social skills takes time and patience, but with practice and a positive attitude, you can improve and make meaningful connections with others.

Discussion Questions: (Please limit to 4-5 questions that pertain to your group)

- Why are social skills important in our daily lives?
- How can practicing empathy improve our social skills and relationships with others?
- Why is it important to seek help from trusted adults or mentors when facing challenges with social skills?
- How can participating in clubs or group activities help improve social skills?
- Reflect on the statement, "Building social skills takes time and patience." Do you agree or disagree?
- Are there any additional tips that you can add to the list provided in the text?
- How do you think practicing kindness and respect can positively impact social interactions within a school or community?

INFORMATION FOR INSTRUCTORS

Barriers to gaining social skills can be hurdles that make it tough to connect with others. Here are some common ones:

- Shyness: Feeling nervous or self-conscious around people can make it hard to initiate conversations or join in activities.
- Low Self-esteem: If you don't feel good about yourself, it can be challenging to believe that others will want to be friends with you.
- Difficulty Reading Social Cues: Not being able to understand facial expressions, body language, or tone of voice can make it tough to know how to respond in social situations.
- Fear of Rejection: Being afraid that others might not like you or might exclude you can hold you back from reaching out to make friends.
- Lack of Social Opportunities: Sometimes, not having many chances to interact with others outside of school or home can make it hard to develop social skills.
- Bullying or Teasing: Being picked on or teased by others can make you hesitant to trust and connect with new people.
- Overwhelm: Feeling overwhelmed by too much social interaction or by big groups of people can make it challenging to engage and participate.

These barriers can make it tough to develop social skills, but with patience, practice, and support from friends, family, or mentors, it's possible to overcome them and build strong social connections.

SUGGESTED GAME: COOKIES FOR THE CONGREGATION!

Bake cookies to give away after church. It encourages the group to work together and engage in an act of service by handing our cookies after service on Sunday.

NOTES:

Printed in the USA
CPSIA information can be obtained
at www.ICGtesting.com
LVHW060914280424
778181LV00023B/127